Profit Dynamics
Achieving Consistent Bottom Line Results

Profit Dynamics
Achieving Consistent Bottom Line Results
John A. Tracy

Dow Jones-Irwin
Homewood, Illinois 60430

For
Big Jack

© RICHARD D. IRWIN, INC., 1989
Dow Jones-Irwin is a trademark of Dow Jones & Company, Inc.
All rights reserved. No part of this publication may be
reproduced, stored in a retrieval system, or transmitted,
in any form or by any means, electronic, mechanical,
photocopying, recording, or otherwise, without the prior
written permission of the publisher.

This publication is designed to provide accurate and
authoritative information in regard to the subject matter
covered. It is sold with the understanding that the
publisher is not engaged in rendering legal, accounting, or
other professional service. If legal advice or other expert
assistance is required, the services of a competent
professional person should be sought.

*From a Declaration of Principles jointly adopted by a Committee
of the American Bar Association and a Committee of Publishers.*

Sponsoring editor: Jim Childs
Project editor: Jane Lightell
Production manager: Ann Cassady
Compositor: Carlisle Communications, Ltd.
Typeface: 11/13 Century Schoolbook
Printer: Arcata Graphics/Kingsport

Library of Congress Cataloging-in-Publication Data
Tracy, John A.
    Profit dynamics.
    Includes index.
    1. Corporate profits.   2. Finance—Decision making.
I. Title.
HG4028.P7T73 1989   658.1'55   88–25634
ISBN 1-55623-110-5

Printed in the United States of America
1 2 3 4 5 6 7 8 9 0 K 5 4 3 2 1 0 9 8

PREFACE

BIRD'S EYE VIEW OF BOOK

Today's business environment is more dynamic than ever before. Managers face constant change, both of their own making and in response to the competition, the economy, and the unexpected. The key factors that drive profit are in constant flux. Managers should know how to estimate the *profit impact* of these changes. Timely analysis is critical. Quick calculations have to be made. Managers need a sure-handed grip on profit.

Good decisions start with good analysis. At decision time the manager needs methods that get right to the answer without sifting through a lot of irrelevant detail. The last few digits of profit depend on a multitude of details. But the *significant* digits depend on a relatively few crucial factors. Even a small change in one factor may cause a huge difference in profit or a swing from profit to loss.

The first part of the book demonstrates how to use certain basic profit analysis techniques. These are the most useful ones for the everyday profit decisions managers have to make. Managers have to crank some numbers, but at the same time should avoid what has been called "analysis paralysis." Calculations should be fast and to the point, although somewhat approximate. Precision is not the objective. Practical examples illustrate each technique without getting too bogged down in detail.

Next, the book moves on to *assets* and *liabilities*. It would be convenient to look only at profit which is reported in the

Income Statement, and not worry about the Balance Sheet which summarizes assets and liabilities. Profit is revenue less expenses, as you undoubtedly know. But, as Paul Harvey says, "the rest of the story" is just as interesting and just as important.

Revenue can be an increase in Cash, an increase in Receivables, an increase in some other asset, or even a decrease in a liability. Expenses are more diverse; expenses decrease four or more different assets and increase three or more different liabilities, depending on which particular expense you're talking about. In summary, revenue and expenses set financial condition in perpetual motion.

Cash is the master clearing account; everything moves through cash sooner or later. It's the "sooner or later" that causes the problems. Cash flow from profit depends on the ebb and flow of the several assets and liabilities driven by profit-making operations. When profit moves in one direction, cash flow usually moves in the *opposite* direction! This fundamental point is critical to financial decision making and control.

Assets less operating liabilities must be balanced with an equal amount of capital. Raising capital boils down to decisions between debt and equity, and the risks and benefits of financial leverage. The time value of money—either as the cost of capital or the return on capital—is the key factor in financial decisions. Managers should be sure-footed on this terrain.

The last chapter discusses management control. Decisions start things in motion, but control brings things to a successful conclusion. Good decisions with bad control may be as disastrous as making bad decisions in the first place. The theme of the last chapter is that control has to be coordinated with decision making. Conventional accounting reports do not necessarily resonate with the analysis techniques used by managers in making decisions. Managers may have to insist on better control reports.

Making profit, of course, is not simply a matter of good analysis and good control. Any business manager will tell you there are many dimensions of success. The manager needs many skills, to be sure. This book concentrates on one essential skill—mastering the basic analytic techniques needed in making profit and financial decisions.

WHOM THE BOOK IS FOR

This book does not require an MBA in Finance. You don't have to be a CPA to understand the book. Just the opposite! The book assumes you have little or no background in accounting and finance. You may have some experience with financial reports and accounting statements. If so, you may have developed a bad attitude toward accountants, and make the wrong assumption that you'll see more of the same in this book. You won't.

This a *not* a book on financial statement analysis, *nor* how to interpret accounting reports. I'm a CPA and have written a successful book on understanding financial reports.[1] I appreciate the problems managers have in dealing with accounting information and the general inability of accountants to communicate clearly and concisely. Accountants are very reluctant to abandon their forbidding technical jargon in reporting to managers, or to anyone else for that matter.

Don't confuse *decision* information and how you analyze this information with the information in accounting statements and how you read such information. Frankly, conventional accounting is not all that relevant for decision making. Accounting provides the historical point of departure for decision information and not much more.

Accounting is *post-decision* oriented. The accounting system accumulates and reports the results of transactions already completed. Keep in mind that the transactions are the end results of decisions made sometime ago. Accounting control information is absolutely essential, of course. Managers must compare the actual results of their decisions against the results originally intended when the decisions were made. You have to know how you're doing and compare this against some benchmark of performance. And managers certainly need to know what's happening that wasn't anticipated. The role of accounting in management control certainly deserves a chapter in the book. But control is not decision making.

---

[1] *How To Read A Financial Report,* 2d ed. John A. Tracy, (New York: John Wiley & Sons, 1983).

To re-emphasize: *At decision time* managers should restrict their attention to the truly important factors which are relatively few, and know how to analyze the main effects of changes in these factors. If analysis mistakes are made at decision time, the final results won't be good. Managers have to get off on the right analytical foot, which is the main thrust of this book.

THE PROFIT MOTIVE

In this book the economic role of profit is taken for granted. Profit stimulates innovation; it's the reward for taking risks; it's the return on equity capital invested in business; it's compensation for hard work and long hours; it motivates efficiency; it weeds out products and services no longer in demand. In short, the profit system delivers the highest standard of living in the world. Despite this, many have a deep-seated bias against profit or are ignorant of the purposes of the profit motive.

But it would be naive to ignore the misuse and failings of the profit motive and the profit-at-any-cost attitude: dishonest advertising, selling unsafe products, cheating employees out of their pensions, unsafe working conditions, and the deliberate violation of laws and regulations and other illegal activities. No wonder profit is a dirty word to so many and why business gets some bad press. Higher ethical standards are a worthy goal never to lose sight of.

DO YOU USE A SPREADSHEET?

You may use a spreadsheet program such as LOTUS 1-2-3 or Excel. If so, you'll find the book especially useful. Most of the examples throughout the chapters are presented in a spreadsheet format. Several places in the book, I mention that I used a spreadsheet to structure and do the computations for the example. I found spreadsheets to be very helpful, and I know you will, too.

Of course, you don't need to know the first thing about spreadsheets to follow the examples. But, if you're a regular user of a spreadsheet, you can easily duplicate the example in your own spreadsheet. It will take only a little time to enter the data. It's not important that you format the output in exactly the same manner as shown in the book. Once you set up your own spreadsheet for an example, you can then easily adapt the example to fit your particular decision situation. As you go through the book, you can build up a collection of those spreadsheets most helpful to you.

ACKNOWLEDGMENTS

An author should never get all the credit for a book. I sincerely thank my editor, Jim Childs, for his very helpful suggestions and contributions. The book is much better for his attention and encouragement. Also, I would like to thank Brad Fishburne very much for his indispensable role in "sponsoring" this book and recommending it to Dow Jones-Irwin. Brad, I owe you one. Last, I would also like to thank all those professionals with Dow Jones-Irwin, from copyediting through final production and promotion, for a top quality effort.

My only regret is that my father, "Big Jack," is not alive to read the book. A long-time business owner and manager, he would have liked the book I think.

CONTENTS

PART I BASICS OF MAKING PROFIT 1

CHAPTER 1 Pathway to Profit 3

Pathway to Operating Profit. A Delicious Example. The Starting Point—Profit Margin Per Unit. Computing Operating Profit. The Break-Even Hurdle. Break-Even as the Starting Point for Computing Operating Profit. Another View of Operating Profit. Why No Income Statement? Summing Up: A Profit Profile for Decision Making.

CHAPTER 2 Profit Sensitivity 16

Constant Change. Sales-Volume Changes. Sales-Price Changes. Product-Cost Changes. Other Changes. Summary

CHAPTER 3 Tough Trade-Offs 29

Sales-Price and Sales-Volume Trade-Offs. Product-Cost, Sales-Price, and Sales-Volume Changes. Changes in Fixed Expenses. Summary

CHAPTER 4 Fine-Tuning the Profit Profile — 45

A Look Ahead. A Few Words About Product Cost. Sales-Revenue-Dependent Expenses. Service Businesses. No Common Denominator of Sales Volume? Summary

CHAPTER 5 Product Cost of Manufacturers — 63

Manufacturers Versus Retailers (and Wholesalers). The Crux of Product Cost: Manufacturing Costs Divided by Production Output. Product Versus Period Costs. Impact of Classification Errors on Operating Profit. Idle Production Capacity. Variable Manufacturing Cost Inefficiencies. Excessive Production. A Final Note: Multiple Products and Overhead-Burden Rates.

CHAPTER 6 Profit Patrol — 82

The Profile of a Loser—or, How to Turn Loss into Profit. The Frustrating Fringe. Sales Mix and Fixed Expenses.

PART II THE FINANCIAL SIDE OF PROFIT — 103

CHAPTER 7 Why You Never See Income Statements Without Balance Sheets — 105

The Balance Sheet and the Income Statement. Basic Impact of Profit on Balance Sheet. A Profit-Making View of the Balance Sheet. A Look Behind and the View Ahead.

CHAPTER 8 Cash Flow — 120

Management Uses of Comparative Balance Sheet. The Cash Flow Statement. Zero Cash Flow from Profit. Summary of Cash Flow from Profit.

CHAPTER 9 Return on Capital   139

Assets and Capital Sources. Completing the Profit Profile and Profiles of Assets Investment and Capital Sources. Improving ROE: The DuPont Model. A Note on Income Tax. Debt and Equity Values: A Final Comment.

CHAPTER 10 Cost of Capital and Time Value of Money   156

The Weighted Average Cost of Capital. Determining the Future Returns Needed from an Asset Investment. Lease or Buy? Notes Receivable from Customers.

PART III A FINAL WORD   175

CHAPTER 11 Management Control   177

What's Ahead. Accounting Controls. Budgeting in Brief. Guidelines for Management Control Reports. A Final Word.

PART 1

BASICS OF MAKING PROFIT

CHAPTER 1

PATHWAY TO PROFIT

How does Coke do it? How does Coca-Cola or any successful business make a profit? The answer is not just making sales, but turning sales revenue into *operating profit*. Over many years Coke's operating profit has stayed very close to 15 percent of its sales revenue. The long-run success of any business is built on the ability of its managers to maintain the operating profit yield, when sales are growing, as well as during downturns. Without doubt, operating profit is the wellspring of a business.

Operating profit is not net income or bottom line profit. Operating profit is profit before deductions for interest and income tax expenses, and before any other unusual (extraordinary) gains and losses during the period. Interest depends how much debt capital is used to finance assets. Sizable amounts of assets are needed to carry on profit-making activity. Before getting into the financial side of the business, managers need a clear picture of operating profit. No part of the picture should be out of focus.

The first several chapters analyze operating profit from the manager's *decision-making* viewpoint. Managers should concentrate first and foremost on making operating profit. Managers must know the pathway to operating profit and avoid detours along the way.

PATHWAY TO OPERATING PROFIT

Operating profit depends on three primary factors: *profit margin, sales volume,* and *fixed expenses.* Managers need a sure-handed grip on these factors. In particular, they must understand the impact of changes in these factors on operating profit. The basic pathway to operating profit is as follows:

Basic Pathway to Operating Profit

Sales Price
(Product Cost)
(Variable Expenses)
 Profit Margin × Sales Volume = Total Profit Margin
 (Fixed Expenses)
 Operating Profit

Profit margin is sales price less product cost and less variable expenses. The first step is setting sales price and controlling product cost and variable expenses, which determine the profit margin per unit. The second step is making sales and achieving sales-volume goals. Profit margin multiplied times sales volume produces the total profit margin needed to overcome fixed expenses and yield operating profit. Tough decisions have to be made every step of the way.

We start with a basic example that walks through the pathway. This walk-through lays the foundation for the essential analysis techniques managers need to reach their profit goals. These basic analysis methods are also a defensive measure, to prevent the mistake of making decisions that may look good until you stop and analyze the profit consequences.

A DELICIOUS EXAMPLE

Everyone likes ice cream, so let's start with an ice cream shop example. Suppose you are thinking of buying an established store that has been in business in a good location for several years. The present owner wants to retire and move to Sun City. He provides the following information for the most recent year. (See Table 1–1).

Selling only single dip cones would not yield $45.00 revenue per gallon. A single dip cone sells for under a dollar and there are 30 scoops per gallon. The basic marketing strategy is to entice customers to "trade up" to sundaes and shakes, which sell for much more than a dollar per scoop.

The purchase cost of the product (ice cream) averages $12.50 per gallon. In addition there are other variable expenses in-

TABLE 1–1
Data For Example

Total sales volume	5,400 gallons
Average sales revenue per gallon	$45.00
Purchase cost per gallon	$12.50
Variable expenses per gallon sold	$2.50
Total fixed expenses for year	$94,500

cluding the cost of cones and cups, plus the toppings, straws, plastic spoons, and napkins. There are a few other variable expenses as well. For example, bad-checks expense varies with the number of sales. The $2.50 per gallon figure includes all the variable expenses.

In contrast to product cost and other variable expenses of making sales, all other operating expenses are *fixed for the year* and do not depend on sales activity. Fixed expenses include a wide variety of costs that the business is committed to for the year. Some are not flexible at all, such as the monthly rent, liability insurance, and depreciation on the store's equipment, furniture, and fixtures. You can see why fixed expenses often are called "overhead."

Some expenses are fixed for the most part, though a bit flexible on the edge. Consider wages expense. The store's employees are paid hourly rates; they are hired either as full-time or half-time employees. So, each employee is paid a fixed wage per week. However, the business could shift to more part-time employees if sales volume dropped off substantially. Conversely, overtime hours could be worked if sales volume surged unexpectedly. For another example, extending the hours the business is open would push the utility bill up some.

To sum up, total fixed expenses were $94,500 last year. This amount would have been much the same even if sales volume had been quite a bit lower or higher.

We'll assume the numbers provided by the seller of the business are reliable and accurate, although you can't be too careful. Before making a final decision to buy the business, you should verify these figures. However, verification might not be too easy. Apply some common sense tests, such as looking at the posted sales prices. Ask to see recent purchase invoices to check the product cost and some of the other variable expenses. Inquire about the reputation of the owner. Ask to see income tax returns for the last two or three years.

For that matter, the seller could be deliberately falsifying the numbers. It happens. I once consulted for a young man thinking of buying a business. He showed me copies of income tax returns for the business. There was one problem. The tax returns were completely phony; the seller got some blank returns and filled in numbers to make things look good. It turned out he made them look too good. The profit margin was far too high for that line of business. I advised my client to hire a CPA to do a quick audit of the records; the seller quickly said the business wasn't for sale after all.

Our ice cream shop illustrates several important points that apply to a very broad cross section of businesses. Every business sets sales prices; every business that sells products has product costs; any business you can think of has some variable expenses tied to sales activity, and virtually every business in the world has fixed expenses. The example may be a little simplified at this point, but it's a good one to build on as we go along.

The present owner has done a very smart thing. He has reduced sales activity to a common denominator—gallons of ice cream. The business sells a wide variety of ice cream products from single dip cones to fancy sundaes with your choice of toppings, to say nothing about the different flavors available which change season to season. But the owner uses gallons as the measure for all sales activity rather than analyzing every different type of sale: by flavor, by single dip, by double dip, or by fancy-versus plain sundae, and so on. For the overall, business-wide analysis of profitability, these details are secondary and would divert attention from the basics.

Suppose the business sold more than just ice cream. Perhaps the store sells souvenir shirts on the side. Of course, you can't mix shirts and gallons of ice cream together into one common denominator of sales volume. Each product line requires a separate column of relevant data as given above for the ice cream product line. For now, we'll limit the example to one product line. This is the basic building block for the multiple product line business. If you can't analyze one product line, you'll certainly have a difficult time with two or more product lines.

TABLE 1–2
Profit Margin Per Unit

Sales revenue per gallon	$ 45.00
Deduct: Product cost per gallon	(12.50)
Variable expenses per gallon	(2.50)
Profit margin per gallon	**$ 30.00**

THE STARTING POINT—PROFIT MARGIN PER UNIT

Based on the information above, how much operating profit did the ice cream shop make last year? To begin, we should compute the most important piece of information **not** given above—the profit margin per gallon of ice cream sold. Note the word "margin;" it's the difference between sales revenue and the direct expenses of bringing in the sales revenue. The profit margin is computed in Table 1–2.

Profit margin per unit is a carefully guarded secret by many businesses. Try calling IBM or General Motors and asking them about their profit margin per computer or per car. In polite but firm language they would tell you to drop dead. On the other hand, unit profit margins for many retailers are widely known; they operate on a standard retail mark-up percent. In our ice cream shop example the unit profit margin is two-thirds of sales revenue ($30.00/$45.00). Other businesses work on much smaller profit margins, as we'll see in later examples.

COMPUTING OPERATING PROFIT

Following the basic pathway given earlier the ice cream shop's operating profit is determined as follows:

Sales Price	$45.00
Product Cost	($12.50)
Variable Expenses	($2.50)
Profit Margin	$30.00
Sales Volume	5,400 gallons
Total Profit Margin	$162,000
Fixed Expenses	($94,500)
Operating Profit	$67,500

The linchpin of this computation is the multiplication of unit profit margin times sales volume to get total profit margin. Sales volume needs a good profit margin per unit to start with. Maybe you've heard the old joke: "A business loses a little on each sale, but makes it up with large volume."

THE BREAK-EVEN HURDLE

Business managers worry a lot about fixed expenses for good reason. There's no operating profit until fixed expenses are overcome. *Break-even* is the crossover point from loss and profit. The *break-even point* is that exact sales volume which multiplied by profit margin per unit gives total profit margin exactly equal to total fixed expenses. At the break-even point, operating profit equals zero. To compute the break-even volume (point) divide total fixed expenses for the year by the profit margin per unit. For this example:

Computation of Break-even Point

Fixed Expenses/Profit Margin per Unit = **Break-even Point**
$94,500/$30.00 = **3,150 gallons**

Go back and "plug in" the sales volume of 3,150 gallons in the computation. Total profit margin would be

$30.00 profit margin per unit × 3,150 gallons = **$94,500**

This is exactly equal to total fixed expenses. So, operating profit would be zero, the break-even point.

Accountants use the term *contribution* margin instead of profit margin to stress the idea that there is no profit until sales volume is sufficient to cover fixed expenses. Their argument is that you don't make any operating profit until you overcome fixed expenses for the period. Making profit depends on getting over the fixed expense hurdle. Fixed expenses may be a tough nut to crack; indeed, sometimes these expenses are called the "nut" of the business.

The following quote from a recent article in *The Wall Street Journal* about Chrysler illustrates the importance of the break-even point. By the way, notice that *vehicles* is the common denominator for its sales volume even though Chrysler makes a wide variety of autos and trucks.

Chrysler's break-even point now stands at 1.8 million vehicles a year, far above the 1.1 million point that Mr. Iacocca vowed to maintain two years ago. The rise isn't entirely alarming—Chrysler sold about 2.3 million vehicles last year, partly because the acquisitions have added to its sales base—but the break-even point is higher than Chrysler would like it to be as it heads into the trough of the industry's sales cycle.[1]

The dead weight nature of fixed expenses is illustrated with the *break-even chart*. Exhibit 1 shows a break-even chart for the ice cream shop example. This is presented as a bar chart instead of a line chart (which is more common) to permit the comparison of total fixed expenses and total profit margin at various sales-volume levels.

EXHIBIT 1–1
Break-even Chart For Ice Cream Shop Example

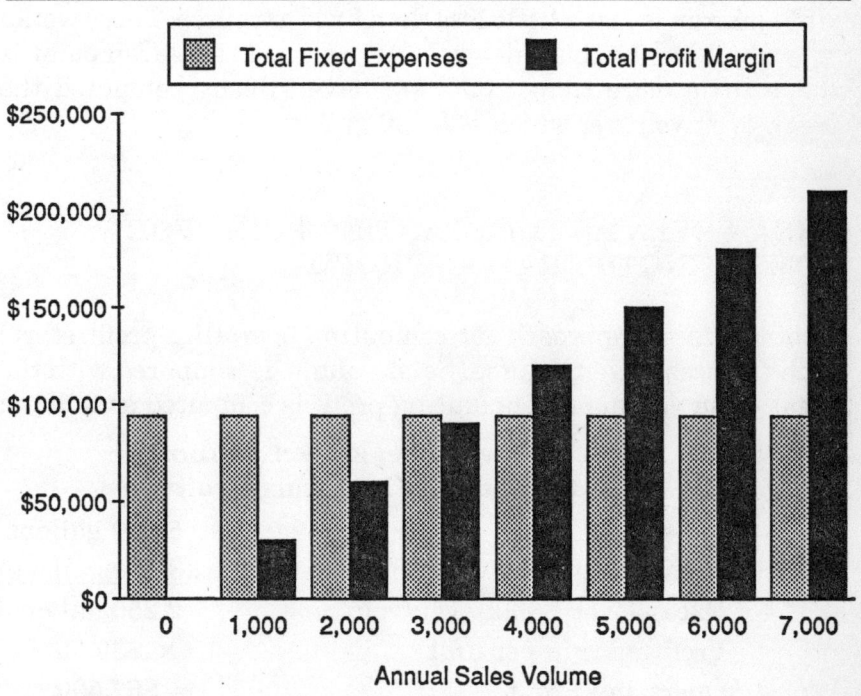

[1] Melinda G. Guiles and Paul Ingrassia, "Yellow Light; Chrysler Hits Brakes, Starts Saving Money After Shopping Spree," *The Wall Street Journal,* January 12, 1988, page 12.

Notice that the fixed expenses column is the same height across all annual sales volumes, from zero to 7,000 gallons. This is the essential aspect of fixed expenses: they remain the same over a very broad span of sales activity. To be more precise, some fixed expenses could be reduced at very low sales levels or might increase at very high sales levels, as already mentioned above. The fixed expenses total is not designed to be precise at the two extremes of sales volumes. Rather, it's accurate over the broad middle of the chart.

The main purpose of the break-even chart is to allow a quick eyeball comparison of total fixed expenses with total profit margin at different sales levels. The total profit margin column increases $30,000 for each 1,000 gallons step-up in annual sales volume:

$30.00 profit margin per gallon × 1,000 gallons = **$30,000**

Look at the 3,000 sales volume level in the Exhibit; the total profit margin is just a little less than fixed expenses. There would be a small loss at this sales volume. So, the break-even point is just a little more than 3,000. We have already computed the break-even volume, which is 3,150 gallons.

BREAK-EVEN AS THE STARTING POINT FOR COMPUTING OPERATING PROFIT

Another useful approach for computing operating profit starts with the break-even volume. Sales volume is compared with the break-even volume and operating profit is computed as follows:

Excess Over Break-even Method of Computing Operating Profit

	Annual-sales volume	5,400 gallons
−	Break-even-sales volume	(3,150 gallons)
=	Excess-over-break-even volume	2,250 gallons
×	Profit-margin per unit	× $30.00
=	Operating Profit	= $67,500

The first 3,150 gallons sold during the year are "assigned" or allocated to cover fixed expenses; the total profit margin from the first 3,150 units is viewed as consumed by fixed expenses. The 2,250 gallons in excess of break-even volume are viewed as the source of operating profit. In other words, sales are divided into two "piles"—the break-even group and the profit group.

Operating profit is the same, although the method of getting there is different. The difference is a little deeper than meets the eye; it's not just an exercise with the numbers, but rather, how to think about making profit in the first place.

The "basic pathway" method of computing operating profit first shown stresses the multiplication of profit margin per unit times sales volume to get total profit margin for the period. Fixed expenses are not ignored, but are simply the final deduction from total profit margin. In contrast, the excess over break-even method just shown puts fixed expenses more in the spotlight, and forces attention on these expenses.

Fixed expenses provide *capacity*. Why else would any rational manager commit to such overhead expenses? In our ice cream shop example fixed expenses buy the space, equipment, and personnel to sell ice cream. Rent on the building, depreciation on the display cabinets and freezers, the wages of employees—with these the business has "bought" a certain amount of *sales capacity*.

The manager should estimate this maximum sales volume and compare this capacity against the 5,400 gallons actual sales volume. Does the business have *excess* or *unused* sales capacity? Could it grow 10, 20, 30 percent before more space would have to be rented, more persons hired, or more equipment installed?

Estimating sales capacity for the ice cream shop may not be all that easy. But a reasonable or ball park estimate can be made. You can start by asking whether a 10 percent increase in sales volume (from 5,400 to 5,940 gallons per year) would require any increase in the total fixed expenses. Maybe not. This is especially important for planning ahead and analyzing the profit impact of changes, which we discuss in the next chapter.

ANOTHER VIEW OF OPERATING PROFIT

Recall that the excess over break-even method divides sales volume into two piles—the quantity necessary to cover total fixed expenses and thus to break-even, and the remainder over the break-even volume which provides operating profit. A third basic method of analyzing operating profit divides *every unit* sold into two parts.

The basic concept of the third method is that profit derives from spreading fixed expenses over enough sales volume so that the average fixed expense per unit is less than the profit margin per unit. The fundamental thinking is that every unit sold has to do two things: (1) contribute its share for fixed expenses; and (2) provide a profit residual. The steps of computation are as follows:

The Average Per Unit Method of Computing Operating Profit

First Step: Compute the average fixes expense per gallon sold.

Total Fixed Expenses/Annual Sales Volume =
Average Fixed Expenses Per Unit Sold
$94,500/5,400 gallons = **$17.50**

Second Step: Compute the difference between the average fixed expenses per unit and the profit margin per unit, and multiple by annual sales volume.

	Profit margin per gallon sold	$30.00
−	Average fixed expenses per gallon	$(17.50)
=	Average operating profit per gallon	$12.50
×	Sales volume	× 5,400 gallons
=	Operating Profit	**$67,500**

As mentioned above, this method spreads the fixed expenses for the year over all units sold, which gives $17.50 per gallon. Profit is viewed as the spread between this average cost and the profit margin per unit of $30.00. So, the business makes $12.50 operating profit per gallon. Each gallon sold is viewed on equal terms—on the order of the "one gallon, one vote" idea.

Suppose the business had sold only 3,150 gallons (which we already know is the break-even volume). Then the average fixed expenses per gallon sold would have been much higher. In fact, it would have been $30.00 per gallon:

$94,500 total fixed expenses/3,150 gallons = **$30.00**

This is exactly equal to the profit margin per unit of $30.00. So, the business would have made precisely zero profit per unit; total operating profit would be zero, which is the break-even point.

WHY NO INCOME STATEMENT?

No Income Statement has been shown in the chapter. So about now you might expect to see one. But you won't. Let me explain. One of the primary functions of accounting is to measure and report profit. Profit reports are prepared for and sent to *three very different* groups: (1) the creditors and stockholders (equity holders) of the business; (2) the managers of the business; and, (3) federal and state income tax agencies. Each receives very different reports.

Profit reports sent to creditors and stockholders are called *Income Statements.* These external profit reports summarize sales revenue and expenses for the year. (Much briefer quarterly reports are also reported.) The key work here is *summarize;* a lot of detail is collapsed and telescoped into a relatively few lines in external Income Statements. External financial statements are bound by many rules and conventions, the most important of which are generally accepted accounting principles, or "GAAP" as accountants affectionately call them. GAAP are the touchstones for external financial statements; deliberate violation of GAAP would constitute fraudulent financial reporting. Managers definitely should understand the basic problems of measuring profit. These financial reporting problems are beyond the scope of this book.

External Income Statements do *not* serve managers very well. These statements conceal as much as they reveal. One of the most basic (though unwritten) rules is that a business does not have to tell all in its external Income Statements. The business has to play fair. But "fair" does not mean that the whole story and the unvarnished truth has to be told. Many details are not reported, such as advertising expense, salaries of top managers, bad-debts expense, inventory shrinkage, and so on. (Even the IRS doesn't require as much Income Statement detail in business income tax returns as you might think.)

It goes without saying that managers need much more detail than reported in external Income Statements. Very detailed internal Profit Performance Reports are indispensable for management *control*. Managers need this feedback information. These statements should highlight deviations from plans and budgets. Management control accounting is discussed in Chapter 11.

But these detailed, internal profit performance reports do not necessarily serve the decision-making needs of managers. Indeed, too much detail works against *decision-making* analysis, and may hinder the manager's ability to focus on the relatively few key factors that drive profit. Also, too much detail works against updating the key profit factors. The more details that have to be up-dated, the less likely the manager will find the time to do it. Last, too much detail obscures the basic relationships and interactions among the primary factors.

SUMMING UP: A PROFIT PROFILE FOR DECISION MAKING

Managers need a short and sweet *Profit Profile* that's quick to use and easy to keep up-to-date: one that follows the basic pathway to profit, and one that shows break-even volume and per unit values. There's no standard format for such a decision-oriented Profit Profile, but I like the following one (See Table 1–3). It's an excellent framework for determining the effects of changes in the primary factors that drive profit, as we explore in the next two chapters.

Compared with conventional Income Statements, the main differences are the following. Both actual sales volume and break-even volume are included. Per unit values are included. Variable operating expenses are separated from fixed operating expenses. None of this information is disclosed in external Income Statements. In external Income Statements only product cost (cost of goods sold) is deducted from sales revenue to get gross profit (or gross margin). But for management decision making, variable operating expenses should also be deducted to get profit margin.

You'll find that the Profit Profile is very helpful. We'll use it frequently in the following chapters. By the way, if you reg-

TABLE 1–3
Profit Profile

	Per Unit	Total
Annual-Break-even Volume		3,150 gallons
Annual-Sales Volume		5,400 gallons
Sales Revenue	$ 45.00	$243,000
Less: Product Cost	$(12.50)	$ (67,500)
Variable Expenses	$ (2.50)	$ (13,500)
Equals: Profit Margin	$ 30.00	$162,000
Less: Fixed Expenses		$ (94,500)
Equals: Operating Profit		$ 67,500

ularly use a spreadsheet program, the Profit Profile is a good place to begin. We'll be using the basic layout of the Profit Profile in the following chapters, so you may want to create your own duplicate of the Profit Profile right now and have it ready to use as we go along.

CHAPTER 2

PROFIT SENSITIVITY

CONSTANT CHANGE

Suppliers may increase the purchase costs of your products; you may increase wage rates for some or all of your employees; the landlord may raise your rent; competitors may drop their prices and you follow them down. All the factors that determine operating profit are subject to change. Business managers face constant change. A basic function of management is to keep a close watch on those changes that impact on the business. The changes set in motion a new round of decisions.

The Profit Profile introduced at the end of Chapter 1 is an excellent framework for assessing the impact of changes and helping to decide the best plan of action in response to changes. In this chapter we analyze changes in each primary factor—**one at a time**—to isolate the impact of that particular factor. In the next chapter we examine the joint effects of changes in two or more factors which often interact in opposite directions (for example, sales prices and sales volume).

Which would you prefer: a 10 percent increase in sales prices or a 10 percent sales volume increase? Is there much difference in operating profit between the two? Suppose your goal is to earn 10 percent more profit next year. How much would you have to increase sales prices? Alternatively, how much more sales volume would be necessary? You may be surprised by some of the answers.

SALES-VOLUME CHANGES

Business managers, quite naturally, are very sales oriented. No sales, no business—it's as simple as that. Many businesses do not make it through their start-up phase because it's very difficult to build up and establish a sales base. But once established, sales volume can never be taken for granted. Sales volume is always vulnerable to competition and shifts in spending decisions by your customers. On the more positive side, sales growth is the most obvious way to increase profit. Managers, in short, have to know the impact of both sales volume decreases and increases.

Ten Percent Sales-Volume Increase

The ice cream shop example introduced in Chapter 1 is carried forward in this chapter. Suppose the annual sales volume increases 10 percent, from 5,400 to 5,940 gallons or an increase of 540 gallons.

Any business manager will tell you there's no such thing as a free lunch. An experienced manager would be a little skeptical here and probably would ask a very good question: *How did the business increase its sales volume?* Did 10 percent more customers just happen to walk into the store, without any increase in advertising, without any cuts in sales prices, without remodeling the store? Possible, but not too likely. Sales volume growth requires some stimulant such as new or more advertising, sales price reductions, etc. Changes in two or more factors are analyzed in Chapter 3. This chapter looks at only one change at a time in order to lay the essential groundwork.

In this example the business makes $30.00 profit margin per gallon. (You may want to refer to the basic Profit Profile introduced at the close of Chapter 1 for a quick review of the data.) The increase in total profit margin from selling 540 additional gallons is straight-forward:

Increase in Total Profit Margin from 10% Sales-Volume Increase

$30.00	× 540	= $16,200
Profit Margin Per Unit	Gallons Increase	Total Profit Margin Increase

18   Basics of Making Profit

A 10 percent sales volume increase raises the question whether the business has enough capacity to handle the additional sales traffic. We'll assume that the business does have enough unused or idle sales capacity to take on 10 percent additional sales volume without any increase in its fixed expenses. However, it's always a good idea to run a capacity check whenever you're looking at an increase in sales volume. In other situations, total fixed expenses may have to be increased to provide the additional sales capacity needed for the sales volume growth.

Table 2–1 summarizes the changes caused by the 10 percent sales volume increase:

Only the items that change are entered in the Profit Profile changes columns. As you can see, none of the per unit values changes neither does total fixed expenses. Also there's no change in the break-even point. Neither the profit margin nor fixed expenses changes so the break-even point stays the same. The margin of safety (the excess of sales volume over break-even volume) is larger at the higher sales volume.

Total sales revenue, total product cost, total variable expenses, and total profit margin all increase 10 percent because sales volume increases 10 percent. The $24,300 sales revenue increase is offset by increases in product cost and variable expenses, resulting in the $16,200 total profit margin increase.

TABLE 2–1
Profit Profile For 10% Sales-Volume Increase

	Before-Sales-Volume Increase		Changes	
Break-even Volume	3,150 gallons			
Sales Volume	5,400 gallons		540 gallons	
	Per Unit	Total	Per Unit	Total
Sales Revenue	$ 45.00	$243,000		$24,300
Product Cost	$(12.50)	$ (67,500)		$ (6,750)
Variable Expenses	$ (2.50)	$ (13,500)		$ (1,350)
Profit Margin	$ 30.00	$162,000		$16,200
Fixed Expenses		$ (94,500)		
Operating Profit		$ 67,500		$16,200

Ten Percent Sales-Volume Decrease

Suppose the ice cream shop suffers a 10 percent sales volume decrease. As manager you should be very concerned, and probe into the reasons for the decrease. More competition? People switching to frozen yogurt away from ice cream? Hard times forcing customers to spend less on ice cream? Location deteriorating? Lousy service to your customers? In any case, you should know the profit impact from the sales decline.

Ten percent less sales volume means 540 fewer gallons are sold. Since each gallon earns $30.00 profit margin, the business would suffer a $16,200 decrease in total profit margin. Fixed expenses would not go down on the lower sales volume. Lowering fixed expenses usually means the business has to make a decision to downsize its sales capacity, which is not easy to accomplish in the short-run.

Table 2–2 summarizes the changes caused by the 10 percent sales volume decrease.

Sales revenue falls off $24,300, but both product cost and variable expenses also decline, so the drop in total profit margin is only $16,200. The 10 percent decrease situation is just the mirror image of the 10 percent increase. In both situations operating profit changes $16,200.

TABLE 2–2
Profit Profile For 10% Sales-Volume Decrease

	Before-Sales-Volume Decrease		Changes	
Break-even Volume	3,150 gallons			
Sales Volume	5,400 gallons		−540 gallons	
	Per Unit	*Total*	*Per Unit*	*Total*
Sales Revenue	$ 45.00	$ 243,000		$(24,300)
Product Cost	$(12.50)	$ (67,500)		$ 6,750
Variable Expenses	$ (2.50)	$ (13,500)		$ 1,350
Profit Margin	$ 30.00	$ 162,000		$(16,200)
Fixed Expenses		$ (94,500)		
Operating Profit		$ 67,500		$(16,200)

Why The Percent Change in Operating Profit Is Much More Than The Percent Change in Sales Volume

Did you happen to notice that operating profit does **not** change by 10 percent? Indeed not. Operating profit changes 24 percent:

$16,200 change/$67,500 operating profit = **24%** *change*

A 10 percent change in sales volume causes a 24 percent change in total profit; there's a multiplier effect on operating profit. What's the reason for this?

The excess over break-even method discussed in Chapter 1 provides the answer. Recall that the first 3,150 units of sales are necessary to cover fixed expenses for the year, which is called the "break-even pile." Operating profit "comes from" the 2,250 units in excess of break-even sold at $30.00 profit margin per unit:

$30.00 × 2,250 units over breakeven
= **$67,500** operating profit.

The "profit pile" provides the operating profit.

Notice what happens in the 10 percent sales volume decrease situation. The decrease of 540 units sold is a 24 percent decrease from the 2,250 profit pile of sales:

540 fewer units sold/2,250 units of profit pile = −24%

You lose 24 percent of the units making profit for you. So, total profit takes a big hit of 24 percent. In the sales volume increase case, the additional 540 units sold is an increase of 24 percent to the profit pile, so operating profit increases 24 percent.

Improving Operating Profit Ten Percent

Suppose your goal is to improve operating profit 10 percent by increasing sales volume; no other factors would be changed, only sales volume. How much would you have to increase sales volume? How many units? What percent?

A 10 percent increase takes operating profit up to $74,250:

$67,500 present operating profit × 110% = **$74,250**

In other words, you need an increase of $6,750. Each unit sold earns $30.00 profit margin. So, you need to sell an additional 225 gallons of ice cream:

$6,750 increase/$30.00 profit margin = **225** more units

Table 2-3 summarizes the increase of 225 units. As you can see operating profit increases $6,750, or 10 percent.

Notice that 225 units is only a little more than a 4 percent increase in sales volume. Here's the multiplier effect again. A 4+ percent sales volume increase produces a 10 percent increase in operating profit. Why? Go back to the "profit pile" again, which is 2,250 units (in excess of the break-even point). To get 10 percent more profit you need 10 percent more of these units:

2,250 profit pile × 10% = **225** additional units

SALES-PRICE CHANGES

Setting sales prices is one of the most difficult decisions facing managers. Competition may dictate the basic range of sales prices. But, usually, there is some room to deviate from your competitor's prices because of product differentiation, location, quality of service, and several other factors. Sales price changes have a big impact on profit.

TABLE 2-3
Profit Profile For 10% Operating-Profit Increase

	Before-Sales-Volume Increase		Changes	
Break-even Volume	3,150 gallons			
Sales Volume	5,400 gallons		225 gallons	
	Per Unit	Total	Per Unit	Total
Sales Revenue	$ 45.00	$ 243,000		$ 10,125
Product Cost	$(12.50)	$ (67,500)		$ (2,813)
Variable Expenses	$ (2.50)	$ (13,500)		$ (562)
Profit Margin	$ 30.00	$ 162,000		$ 6,750
Fixed Expenses		$ (94,500)		
Operating Profit		$ 67,500		$ 6,750

Increasing Sales Prices Ten Percent

What would happen to operating profit if you increase sales prices 10 percent? Admittedly, this is a relatively big step up. Price increases of this magnitude don't go unnoticed by customers. Obviously, sales volume might drop, which we examine in the next chapter. Here we are concerned with the effects of the sales price increase and only this change.

Is the operating profit impact of a 10 percent sales price increase noticeably more than the 10 percent sales volume increase? Or, would it produce about the same result? The sales price increase would be much better, as shown in Table 2–4. As you can see, operating profit increases $24,300 for a 36 percent increase:

$24,300 increase/$67,500 operating profit = **36%**.

Here's the multiplier effect again; a 10 percent increase in sales prices drives up profit by more than one-third! Why?

Each unit sold brings in $4.50 more revenue *without increases in product cost or other variable expenses*. Thus:

5,400 gallons sold × $4.50 profit margin increase = **$24,300**

Notice also that the profit margin per unit goes from $30.00 to $34.50; this increase lowers the break-even point by 411 units or to 2,739 gallons.

TABLE 2–4
Profit Profile For 10% Sales-Price Increase

	Before-Sales-Price Increase		*Changes*	
Break-even Volume	3,150 gallons		−411 gallons	
Sales Volume	5,400 gallons			
	Per Unit	Total	Per Unit	Total
Sales Revenue	$ 45.00	$243,000	$4.50	$24,300
Product Cost	$(12.50)	$ (67,500)		
Variable Expenses	$ (2.50)	$ (13,500)		
Profit Margin	$ 30.00	$162,000	$4.50	$24,300
Fixed Expenses		$ (94,500)		
Operating Profit		$ 67,500		$24,300

The key difference between a sales-price increase and a sales-volume increase can be spotted by comparing the profit profiles for each case. In both situations sales revenue goes up $24,300. In the sales volume increase case, the product cost and variable expenses also go up for a net increase in operating profit of only $16,200. In contrast, in the sales-price increase case **all** the $24,300 of additional sales revenue flows through to operating profit.

Decreasing Sales Prices Ten Percent

What goes up can go down; consider a 10 percent sales price decrease. This hurts as much as the sales-price increase helps. Managers should always keep in mind the rather disastrous effects of decreasing sales prices. It takes a very large sales-volume increase to offset such effects, which we examine in the next chapter. A 10 percent sales-volume increase does not even come close to offsetting a 10 percent sales-price decrease. Here we will look at the damage done by the 10 percent sales-price decrease assuming sales volume remains the same.

The Profit Profile for this situation is shown in Table 2–5. As you might have anticipated, operating profit drops $24,300 for a 36 percent plunge. Each unit brings in $4.50 less sales revenue, so:

5,400 gallons sold × $4.50 profit margin decrease = −$24,300

TABLE 2–5
Profit Profile For 10% Sales-Price Decrease

	Before-Sales-Price Decrease		Changes	
Break-even Volume	3,150 gallons		556 gallons	
Sales Volume	5,400 gallons			
	Per Unit	Total	Per Unit	Total
Sales Revenue	$ 45.00	$ 243,000	$(4.50)	$(24,300)
Product Cost	$(12.50)	$ (67,500)		
Variable Expenses	$ (2.50)	$ (13,500)		
Profit Margin	$ 30.00	$ 162,000	$(4.50)	$(24,300)
Fixed Expenses		$ (94,500)		
Operating Profit		$ 67,500		$(24,300)

Notice also that the break-even volume increases 556 gallons because the unit profit margin decreases from $30.00 to $25.50 per unit.

Improving Operating Profit Ten Percent

Suppose your goal is to improve operating profit 10 percent by increasing sales prices exactly enough to achieve this objective. How much do you have to increase sales revenue per gallon? What percent increase is this?

You want to increase operating profit 10 percent of $67,500 or $6,750, up to $74,250. Only the sales revenue per gallon changes; all other factors remain the same. You have to get $6,750 more total sales revenue from 5,400 gallons:

$6,750 increase/5,400 gallons = $1.25 more revenue per unit

The sales revenue has to be raised to $46.25 per gallon. Table 2–6 shows that this new sales revenue per gallon would give the desired result. (Notice also that the break-even point decreases a little because of the increase in profit margin per unit.)

TABLE 2–6
Profit Profile For 10% Profit Improvement

	Before-Sales Price Increase		Changes	
Break-even Volume	3,150 gallons		−126 gallons	
Sales Volume	5,400 gallons			
	Per Unit	Total	Per Unit	Total
Sales Revenue	$ 45.00	$ 243,000	$1.25	$6,750
Product Cost	$(12.50)	$ (67,500)		
Variable Expenses	$ (2.50)	$ (13,500)		
Profit Margin	$ 30.00	$ 162,000	$1.25	$6,750
Fixed Expenses		$ (94,500)		
Operating Profit		$ 67,500		$6,750

PRODUCT-COST CHANGES

Sales volume and sales price are the two factors having the most obvious impact on operating profit. Product cost would rank next for most businesses. Managers should be on top of product-cost changes as well as the other basic profit factors.

Purchasing can be slighted in overall business profit planning and control. It can be carried to an extreme. I know a purchasing agent who was a neighbor when I lived in California some years ago. He was a real tiger. For instance, he would even return calendars sent by vendors at the end of the year with a note saying, "Don't send me this calendar; give me a lower price." This may seem to be overkill, but he eventually became General Manager of the business.

Suppose the creamery just notified the business that the cost per gallon of ice cream will increase 10 percent. As before, assume all other factors remain the same. The impact of the product cost increase is shown in the Table 2-7.

Notice that the product cost increases 10 percent or $1.25 per gallon. How much damage does this cause? Each gallon sold brings in $1.25 less profit margin for $6,750 less total profit margin:

$1.25 less profit margin × 5,400 gallons = −$6,750

TABLE 2-7
Profit Profile For 10% Product-Cost Increase

	Before-Product-Cost Increase		Changes	
Break-even Volume	3,150 gallons		137 gallons	
Sales Volume	5,400 gallons			
	Per Unit	Total	Per Unit	Total
Sales Revenue	$ 45.00	$ 243,000		
Product Cost	$(12.50)	$ (67,500)	$(1.25)	$(6,750)
Variable Expenses	$ (2.50)	$ (13,500)		
Profit Margin	$ 30.00	$ 162,000	$(1.25)	$(6,750)
Fixed Expenses		$ (94,500)		
Operating Profit		$ 67,500		$(6,750)

Also, the break-even point increases slightly because the profit margin per unit drops from $30.00 to $28.75.

In the next chapter we consider the case in which the manager has to figure out how much sales prices should be increased to offset a product-cost increase. It would seem this is fairly simple, but there are some other factors that make it a little more complex than meets the eye. We will not go through the product cost decrease case here. It would, of course, have the opposite effect of the increase situation.

OTHER CHANGES

The remaining two factors—variable expenses per unit and total fixed expenses—are covered very quickly. The costs of straws, napkins, cones, etc. will fluctuate. Likewise, any of the many items making up total fixed expenses is subject to change. Rent may increase, insurance may go down (not too likely, I suppose), utility bills go up, and so on. Two situations are shown below for a 10 percent decrease in variable expenses per unit and a 10 percent increase in total fixed expenses.

The effects of a 10 percent decrease in variable expenses per unit are shown in Table 2–8.

TABLE 2–8
Profit Profile For 10% Variable-Expenses Decrease

	Before-Variable-Expense Decrease		Changes	
Break-even Volume	3,150 gallons		−26 gallons	
Sales Volume	5,400 gallons			
	Per Unit	Total	Per Unit	Total
Sales Revenue	$ 45.00	$ 243,000		
Product Cost	$(12.50)	$ (67,500)		
Variable Expenses	$ (2.50)	$ (13,500)	$0.25	$1,350
Profit Margin	$ 30.00	$ 162,000	$0.25	$1,350
Fixed Expenses		$ (94,500)		
Operating Profit		$ 67,500		$1,350

The effects of a 10 percent increase in total fixed expenses are as shown in Table 2–9.

As you can see a 10 percent increase in fixed expenses has more than one undesirable effect. Not only is operating profit reduced $9,450, but the break-even point is increased. On the plus side notice that the profit margin per unit and total profit margin are not changed. To bring operating profit back up to the level before the change, either the profit margin per unit or the sales volume, or some combination of both has to be improved.

SUMMARY

This chapter analyzes the effects of 10 percent changes in each of the primary factors that drives operating profit performance. If you had your choice, the best change is the 10 percent sales-price increase which yields the largest operating profit increase. The 10 percent volume increase is second. A sales-price increase is **always** better than an equal percent sales-volume increase. Sales volume and sales prices are the "two big" factors. But no factor should be overlooked.

All the factors are subject to change. Management neglect or ineptitude can lead to deterioration in the factors, sometimes

TABLE 2–9
Profit Profile For 10% Fixed-Expenses Increase

	Before-Fixed-Expenses Increase		Changes	
Break-even Volume	3,150 gallons		315 gallons	
Sales Volume	5,400 gallons			
	Per Unit	Total	Per Unit	Total
Sales Revenue	$ 45.00	$ 243,000		
Product Cost	$(12.50)	$ (67,500)		
Variable Expenses	$ (2.50)	$ (13,500)		
Profit Margin	$ 30.00	$ 162,000		
Fixed Expenses		$ (94,500)		$(9,450)
Operating Profit		$ 67,500		$(9,450)

very quickly. To be realistic, managers may not be able to improve certain factors very much. Fixed expenses may already be cut to the bone. Product costs may be controlled by one vendor; or, alternative vendors may offer virtually the same prices.

Competition may put a fairly tight straightjacket on sales prices. Customers are sensitive to sales-price increases. So, sales volume is the key factor for many businesses. However, increases in product cost and variable and fixed expenses have to be passed along to customers sooner or later.

CHAPTER 3

TOUGH TRADE-OFFS

Typically a change in one primary profit factor leads to or is in response to a change in another factor. Raise your sales prices and sales volume may very well drop. Lower your sales prices and sales volume may increase, unless competitors lower their prices also. Higher sales prices may be in response to higher product costs. Spending more on fixed expenses—for example, bigger advertising budgets, higher rent for bigger stores, or more expensive furnishings—may increase sales volume. None of this is news to the experienced business manager. The business world is one of *trade-offs* among the primary profit factors.

The preceding chapter analyzes changes in one factor at a time; all others are held constant. But in the real world of business seldom can you change just one thing at a time. One change causes another.

In this chapter we analyze the *interaction effects* of changes in two or more factors on operating profit. Suppose a 10 percent sales-price decrease results in a 10 percent sales-volume increase. Would this be a good idea? Would a 10 percent sales-price increase with a 10 percent sales-volume decrease be better? If product cost goes up, should sales prices be increased the same amount to keep operating profit the same? Do you know the answers to such questions? If not, you'd better continue reading.

NEWCO sells a big ticket item with a high sales price, such as personal computers or high-end consumer electronics. Notice that management has made an estimate of the *practical sales capacity* that the business could achieve with its present level of fixed expenses. This is the maximum annual sales volume the business could handle without increasing several of its fixed expenses. Beyond this volume the business would have to expand its space, hire more employees on fixed salaries, buy additional equipment that would increase depreciation expense, and so on (see Table 3–1).

TABLE 3–1
Profit Profile For NEWCO

Annual-Sales Volume	1,000 units	
Annual-Break-even Volume	680 units	
Annual-Capacity Volume	1,250 units	
	Per Unit	Total
Sales Revenue	$ 2,000	$ 2,000,000
Product Cost	$(1,200)	$(1,200,000)
Variable Expenses	$ (300)	$ (300,000)
Profit Margin	$ 500	$ 500,000
Fixed Expenses		$ (340,000)
Operating Profit		$ 160,000

It's very convenient to keep the numbers easy to deal with so you can follow each step in your mind's eye. You'll notice all numbers are rounded off. In practice, managers have to round off the data and make estimates. The Profit Profile is for *planning and decision-making* analysis. In no way does it replace internal profit performance reports that managers depend on for *control* purposes. Control reports contain very detailed, precise historical information in contract to the summarized, future-oriented data in the Profit Profile. (Chapter 11 discusses management control.)

SALES-PRICE AND SALES-VOLUME TRADE-OFFS

Ten Percent Sales-Price Decrease With Ten Percent Sales-Volume Increase—A Terrible Idea

Suppose you're the sales manager of this company. You're seriously thinking of decreasing the sales price 10 percent, which you think would increase sales volume at least 10 percent. Of course, competition may follow you down in price, so the sales-volume increase may not materialize. But you don't think they will. Your product is different from the competition. (Brand names and product specifications are two examples of differences.) There always has been some sales price spread between your product and the competition. A 10 percent price cut should not trigger a price war in your opinion.

One reason for your sales price reduction plan is that the business is not selling up to its capacity. As you see in the Profit Profile for the business, the present sales volume is below capacity. This is not unusual since most businesses have some slack or untapped sales capacity provided by fixed expenses. NEWCO'S fixed expenses provide enough space and personnel to handle up to a 25 percent larger sales volume (see Table 3–1 for the Profit Profile for NEWCO). Rather than down-sizing the space or number of employees, your first thought is to increase sales volume and thus take better advantage of the capacity being paid for by the fixed expenses.

Sales volume may not respond to the reduction in sales price as much as you predict. In contrast, sales volume may increase more than 10 percent. In any case you plan to monitor closely the reaction of customers. If there is not enough sales volume increase you can reverse directions quickly.

Before a final decision is made, wouldn't it be a good idea to see what would happen to operating profit if you're correct about the sales-volume increase? Table 3–2 presents the Profit Profile for the Before and After scenarios; the format is adapted to show volume changes and profit-impact changes.

Whoops! The 10 percent sales-price cut would be a disaster. Assuming the sales-volume projection is correct, the sales-price reduction would wipe out operating profit and cause a *loss*. There would be a negative swing of $170,000—from $160,000 profit to $10,000 *loss*.

First of all, notice that sales volume increases 10 percent (from 1,000 units to 1,100 units) and sales price decreases 10 percent (from $2,000 to $1,800). This is your plan. The other three primary profit factors—product cost per unit, the variable expenses per unit, and total fixed expenses—remain the same. So, why is there such a devastating impact on operating profit?

TABLE 3-2
Profit Profile for 10% Sales-Price Decrease & 10% Sales-Volume Increase

	Before	After	Change
Sales Volume	1,000 units	1,100 units	100
Break-even Volume	680 units	1,133 units	453
Capacity Volume	1,250 units	1,250 units	0

	Per Unit		Total		Profit Impact
	Before	After	Before	After	
Sales Revenue	$ 2,000	$ 1,800	$ 2,000,000	$ 1,980,000	$ (20,000)
Product Cost	$(1,200)	$(1,200)	$(1,200,000)	$(1,320,000)	$(120,000)
Variable Expenses	$ (300)	$ (300)	$ (300,000)	$ (330,000)	$ (30,000)
Profit Margin	$ 500	$ 300	$ 500,000	$ 330,000	$(170,000)
Fixed Expenses			$ (340,000)	$ (340,000)	$ 0
Operating Profit			$ 160,000	$ (10,000)	$(170,000)

Notice what happens to total sales revenue; it actually *decreases* $20,000. Total product cost and total variable expenses increase because sales volume increases 10 percent. The sum of the $20,000 decrease in total sales revenue, plus the increases of $120,000 and $30,000 in total product cost and total variable expenses, results in the $170,000 drop in total profit margin.

Profit margin is the key point. A sales price decrease of 10 percent or $200 per unit is a misleading way to think about your plan. The $200 is a **40** percent decrease in the profit margin per unit:

$200 decrease/$500 profit margin = **40%**

You can't give up 40 percent of your profit margin per unit and make it back with a 10 percent sales-volume increase. (Later we determine what sales volume would keep operating profit the same; it's a lot!)

Because the profit margin per unit goes down so much, the break-even point goes up to over 1,100 units:

$340,000 fixed expenses/$300 profit margin
= 1,133 units to break-even

The business falls below its break-even point, and slips into the red.

In short, the 10 percent trade-off between sales price and sales volume causes a drastic decrease in operating profit. In fact, any trade-off that lowers sales price with an equal percent increase in sales volume decreases operating profit. Total sales revenue will go down and total expenses will go up because of the sales-volume increase. Yet, we see sales price reductions of 10 percent or more all the time. What's going on?

First of all, many sales-price reductions are from **list** prices that no one takes as the final price; list prices are only a point of reference for getting to the real price. This example refers to real prices, or the sales revenue per unit actually received by the business. Can a business cut its real sales price 10 percent and increase profit? Sales volume would have to increase much more than 10 percent, which we'll look at shortly.

Would this 10 percent sales-price/sales-volume trade-off **ever** be a smart move? It would seem not; we have settled this in the analysis above, haven't we? Well, there is one situation that brings up an extremely important point.

Notice one thing in Table 3–2—the product cost per unit remains the same before and after at $1,200 per unit. This assumes that to have products to sell, the business either has to buy (or make) them at this cost, or if already in inventory, the business has to pay this cost to replace the units sold. This is the standard assumption, but may not be true in certain situations.

In particular, a business may not replace the units sold; it may be at the end of the product's life cycle. Perhaps the product is being replaced with a newer model. In this situation the historical, accounting cost of inventory becomes a "sunk cost." This means the cost is like water over the dam; it can't be reversed.

If units held in inventory will not be replaced, in other words, if the business is at the end of the line on these units and is selling off its remaining inventory of the product, then the recorded product cost is not relevant. What the business paid in the past for the units should be disregarded. The decision should ignore product cost and focus on the highest sales price that would move all the units out of inventory.

Sales-Volume Increase Needed To Offset Ten Percent Sales-Price Reduction—A Quick Calculation

How much sales-volume increase would it take to offset the 10 percent sales-price cut? That is, what would sales volume have to be just to keep operating profit the same as before? At the lower sales price, profit margin per unit is only $300. To get up to break-even you need to sell 1,133 units (see Table 3–2). To make $160,000 operating profit you need an additional 533 units over break-even:

$$\$160{,}000 \text{ operating profit}/\$300 \text{ profit margin} = 533 \text{ additional units}$$

So, sales volume would have to reach 1,667 units or 1,133 units to break even plus 533 units to make profit.

The Profit Profile for this sales volume proves this. But I won't bother to show it mainly because the higher sales volume is considerably above the sales capacity of the business (which is only 1,250 units). Fixed expenses would have to be increased, which would be another change to include in the analysis. Fixed expenses are analyzed later.

Ten Percent Sales-Price Increase With Ten Percent Sales-Volume Decrease—Too Good To Be True?

Even though NEWCO has excess sales capacity, suppose you are thinking of a 10 percent sales-price **increase,** knowing that sales volume probably would drop. In fact, you think it will drop at least 10 percent. Sales managers are generally very adverse to any drop in sales volume, especially a loss of market share which could be very difficult to reverse and build back up later. There's no question that any move that decreases sales volume has to be considered very carefully. But, putting aside these warnings, would a sales price hike of 10 percent be a good idea if sales volume dropped 10 percent?

By now you should expect to see the Profit Profile for this scenario, Table 3–3. However, before you look at it, what did you expect? A big increase in operating profit? That big?

TABLE 3–3
Profit Profile for 10% Sales-Price Increase & 10% Sales-Volume Decrease

	Before	After	Change
Sales Volume	1,000 units	900 units	−100
Break-even Volume	680 units	486 units	−194
Capacity Volume	1,250 units	1,250 units	0

	Per Unit		Total		Profit
	Before	After	Before	After	Impact
Sales Revenue	$ 2,000	$ 2,200	$ 2,000,000	$ 1,980,000	$ (20,000)
Product Cost	$(1,200)	$(1,200)	$(1,200,000)	$(1,080,000)	$120,000
Variable Expenses	$ (300)	$ (300)	$ (300,000)	$ (270,000)	$ 30,000
Profit Margin	$ 500	$ 700	$ 500,000	$ 630,000	$130,000
Fixed Expenses			$ (340,000)	$ (340,000)	$ 0
Operating Profit			$ 160,000	$ 290,000	$130,000

Notice that total sales revenue actually decreases $20,000, the same as in the previous case. But, in this situation notice that total product cost decreases $120,000 and total variable expenses decrease $30,000. Total expenses go down $150,000 with only a drop of $20,000 in sales revenue, giving a net increase of $130,000 in total profit margin. You could say that you're giving up $20,000 of revenue to save $150,000 of expenses.

As before, profit margin per unit is the key, which increases from $500 to $700 per unit. Thus the break-even point also decreases. Total fixed expenses stay the same; they certainly wouldn't go up with the decrease in sales volume. If anything, some of these costs possibly could be reduced.

The big increase in operating profit is based on the prediction that sales volume would drop only 10 percent. What if it fell 15, 20, or 25 percent? We can recalculate the Profile Profile for any particular sales volume change.[1] In any case, probably the most relevant question to ask here is how much sales volume

---

[1] It may have already occurred to you that the Profile Profile is a prime candidate for a micro computer spreadsheet program such as LOTUS 1–2–3. As a matter of fact, I have it on an EXCEL spreadsheet program. If you have a spreadsheet program I encourage you to enter the data for the Profit Profile example, and to test your output against mine as we continue.

would have to drop for the 10 percent sales-price increase to cause a decrease in operating profit.

Sales-Volume Decrease That Would Offset Ten Percent Sales-Price Increase

The sales-volume decrease that would offset a 10 percent sales-price increase can be determined as follows: Start with the break-even point; as you can see in Table 3–3, this is 486 units. The operating profit target is $160,000, the same as before the sales price increase. Each unit sold yields $700 profit margin per unit; therefore,

$160,000 operating profit/$700 profit margin = 229 units

The business would have to sell 486 units to break even plus another 229 units to make an operating profit of $160,000 for a total of 714 units. See Table 3–4.

In summary, sales volume could drop 286 units, or about 29 percent before operating profit would be any lower than before. Of course, no one knows for certain how sales volume would respond to a 10 percent sales-price reduction. For that matter,

TABLE 3–4
Profit Profile For The Sales-Volume Decrease That Would Offset 10% Sales-Price Increase

	Before	After	Change
Sales Volume	1,000 units	714 units	−286
Break-even Volume	680 units	486 units	−194
Capacity Volume	1,250 units	1,250 units	0

	Per Unit		Total		Profit Impact
	Before	After	Before	After	
Sales Revenue	$ 2,000	$ 2,200	$ 2,000,000	$1,571,429	$(428,571)
Product Cost	$(1,200)	$(1,200)	$(1,200,000)	$ (857,143)	$ 342,857
Variable Expenses	$ (300)	$ (300)	$ (300,000)	$ (214,286)	$ 85,714
Profit Margin	$ 500	$ 700	$ 500,000	$ 500,000	$ 0
Fixed Expenses			$ (340,000)	$ (340,000)	$ 0
Operating Profit			$ 160,000	$ 160,000	$ 0

sales may not decrease at all. Or sales may drop more than 29 percent. In any case, the Profit Profile provides profit-impact analysis based on the best predictions possible.

PRODUCT-COST, SALES-PRICE, AND SALES-VOLUME CHANGES

Passing Through Product-Cost Increases To Sales Price

If product cost goes up 10 percent or $120 per unit, then all you have to do is to raise the sales price $120 to make the same total operating profit. But the sales-price increase may affect sales volume. Furthermore, there are two quite different reasons for product-cost increases. General inflation may drive up the product cost; the same product costs more because costs in general are going up.

The higher product cost may reflect quality improvements in the product. In this case, the product itself is changed for the better. Customers may be willing to pay more for the improved product with no decrease in sales volume. If the sales price is kept the same, then sales volume may increase.

Consider the first situation: The product is the **same,** but it costs more than before. The supplier of this product just announced a 10 percent price increase from $1,200 to $1,320 per unit. (Or production cost could increase 10 percent if the business were a manufacturer.) The business has to decide how to pass this product-cost increase through to its customers, knowing that the higher sales price may decrease sales volume.

The precise sensitivity of demand to sales price is not known.[2] But the sales manager knows from experience that a higher sales price will have some adverse effect on demand. As a rough rule of thumb, the sales manager assumes that each 1 percent increase of sales price causes an equal 1 percent decrease of sales volume. This may be too conservative; sales volume may not

---

[2] Economists call this "elasticity of demand."

drop this much, especially in a general inflationary environment in which consumers expect everything to go up over time and take price increases in stride. But to decide on the new sales price, the business will use this rule of thumb.

Raising the sales price $120 would be a 6 percent increase based on the old sales price of $2,000. This would mean a 6 percent drop in sales volume. The same profit margin per unit ($500) would be earned on 6 percent fewer units; thus, operating profit would drop. The business wants to set the new sales price so that operating profit would be the same as before. The Profit Profile for this situation is shown in Table 3–5.

Notice that the new sales price is $2,165. As discussed *above*, it is assumed that any increase in the sales price is offset with an equal percent decrease in sales volume. The sales price increases $165, which is an increase of 8.25 percent. So, sales volume goes down this percent—to 918 units (to be precise, to 917.5 units which is rounded to 918 units). At this combination of sales price, sales volume, and product cost—remember that the other primary factors do not change—you can see that operating profit remains the same at $160,000 (see Table 3–5).

TABLE 3–5
Profit Profile For 10% Product-Cost Increase That Is Passed Through In Higher-Sales Price (Causing A Lower-Sales Volume)

	Before		After		Change
Sales Volume	1,000 units		918 units		−82
Break-even Volume	680 units		624 units		−56
Capacity Volume	1,250 units		1,250 units		0
	Per Unit		Total		
	Before	After	Before	After	Profit Impact
Sales Revenue	$ 2,000	$ 2,165	$ 2,000,000	$ 1,986,397	$(13,603)
Product Cost	$(1,200)	$(1,320)	$(1,200,000)	$(1,211,138)	$(11,138)
Variable Expenses	$ (300)	$ (300)	$ (300,000)	$ (275,259)	$ 24,741
Profit Margin	$ 500	$ 545	$ 500,000	$ 500,000	$ 0
Fixed Expenses			$ (340,000)	$ (340,000)	$ 0
Operating Profit			$ 160,000	$ 160,000	$ 0

Determining the exact sales price is not the purpose here. The easiest way to do this is to use a spreadsheet program; keep changing the sales price and the corresponding sales volume until you get exactly the operating profit you want. (Indeed, this is how I did it.) The key point is that a product cost increase cannot be simply added to the sales price if the sales volume, in turn, is affected by the sales-price increase.

The profit profile is an excellent framework to solve for the profit goals of the business, one that keeps all the essential relationships in full view of each other. It displays the entire picture of effects. For instance, notice that the break-even volume drops a little at the higher sales price, and that the profit margin per unit rises to $545.

Notice also that sales volume drops. As mentioned before, sales managers take a very dim view of decreases in sales volume because it may lead to a permanent loss of market share. Hopefully, competitors face the same general inflation in product costs so that sales volume would not suffer from passing along the product-cost increase.

Product-Cost Increases Leading To Sales-Volume Increases

The other basic type of product cost increase involves product improvement. These quality improvements may be part of the marketing strategy to give customers a better product at the same sales price to stimulate demand.

Assume NEWCO's product-cost increases 10 percent because of improvements in the quality of the product. (For that matter, the size of the product may be increased, such as bigger candy bars.) Management has decided *not* to increase the sales price because demand should increase for the improved product. Of course, it goes without saying that this depends on customers being made aware and convinced of the improvements. Before a final decision is made management would like to know just how much sales volume would have to increase to keep operating profit the same.

Each unit sold would earn $120 less profit margin per unit; product cost increases this amount while sales price remains the same. So, the profit margin per unit drops to $380. The break-even sales volume is 895 units:

$340,000 fixed expenses/$380 profit margin = 895 units

To earn operating profit of $160,000 requires additional sales of 421 units (computed the same way) for a total sales volume of 1,316 units (see Table 3-6).

Two things are very bad in this scenario. First, sales volume would have to increase more than 30 percent or 316 units, to be precise. Second, the required sales level is more than capacity. So fixed expenses would have to be increased. Thus, the business may have to rethink its plan not to increase sales price; some increase, even a modest one, might be necessary.

Decreases In Product Cost Or Other Variable Expenses Leading to Sales-Volume Decreases

Suppose the business were able to lower either its product cost or its variable expenses per unit. On the one hand, such savings may be true efficiency gains. The purchase cost may be reduced by sharper bargaining. (If the business is a manufacturer, pro-

TABLE 3-6
Profit Profile For 10% Product-Cost Increase With No Increase In Sales Price But Large Increase In Sales Volume

	Before	After	Change
Sales-Volume	1,000 units	1,316 units	316
Break-even Volume	680 units	895 units	215
Capacity Volume	1,250 units	1,250 units	0

	Per Unit		Total		Profit Impact
	Before	After	Before	After	
Sales Revenue	$ 2,000	$ 2,000	$ 2,000,000	$ 2,631,579	$ 631,579
Product Cost	$(1,200)	$(1,320)	$(1,200,000)	$(1,736,842)	$(536,842)
Variable Expenses	$ (300)	$ (300)	$ (300,000)	$ (394,737)	$ (94,737)
Profit Margin	$ 500	$ 380	$ 500,000	$ 500,000	$ 0
Fixed Expenses			$ (340,000)	$ (340,000)	$ 0
Operating Profit			$ 160,000	$ 160,000	$ 0

ductivity improvements would lower the product cost per unit.) On the other hand, there may be a general deflation of prices. Or wasteful expenses could be eliminated. The key question is whether the product remains the same and whether the quality of service to customers remains the same. Maybe not. Product-cost decreases may represent quality decreases or other "dis-improvements" in the product. Variable expense reductions may adversely affect the quality of service to customers.

In the first case (same product and same service), sales volume should not be affected. Customers would see no differences in the product or service. In the second case (degradation in the quality of the product or service to customers), sales volume may very well drop off somewhat. The first case is the best. Cost savings pass directly through to operating profit. Suppose the business reduces its variable expenses 10 percent or $30 per unit. This cost savings would apply to 1,000 units sold for an operating profit increase of $30,000.

But what if the reduction in variable expenses hurts the quality of service to customers and thus sales volume decreases? In fact, suppose the sales manager predicts that sales volume would drop by 2 percent or so. Table 3–7 shows the Profit Profile for this situation.

TABLE 3–7
Profit Profile For 10% Variable-Expenses Decrease With 2% Decrease In Sales Volume

	Before		After		Change
Sales Volume	1,000 units		980 units		−20
Break-even Volume	680 units		642 units		−38
Capacity Volume	1,250 units		1,250 units		0
	Per Unit		Total		
	Before	After	Before	After	Profit Impact
Sales Revenue	$ 2,000	$ 2,000	$ 2,000,000	$ 1,960,000	$(40,000)
Product Cost	$(1,200)	$(1,200)	$(1,200,000)	$(1,176,000)	$ 24,000
Variable Expenses	$ (300)	$ (270)	$ (300,000)	$ (264,600)	$ 35,400
Profit Margin	$ 500	$ 530	$ 500,000	$ 519,400	$ 19,400
Fixed Expenses			$ (340,000)	$ (340,000)	$ 0
Operating Profit			$ 160,000	$ 179,400	$ 19,400

As you can see, operating profit increases even though sales volume drops 20 units or 2 percent. NEWCO would lose $40,000 sales revenue; but with the drop in sales volume, total product cost also drops $24,000. The *net* effect is a $16,000 decrease in gross profit (sales revenue less cost-of-goods sold). The $35,400 reduction in variable expenses is more than enough to offset the gross profit decrease. But, again it should be mentioned that any loss of sales volume is a serious matter.

We could keep decreasing the sales volume in the Profit Profile to see just how much it would have to fall to hold even on the reduction in variable expenses per unit. This worst case scenario is not shown here. (Sales volume would have to drop to 943 units, which you can check if you like.)

CHANGES IN FIXED EXPENSES

Why do fixed expenses increase? The increase may be due to general inflationary trends; for instance, utility bills or insurance premiums may go up. Or, the fixed expense increase may be the result of a decision to expand capacity; the business could rent a larger space. Or, fixed expenses may increase due to improving the sales value of the present location; the business could invest in better furnishings and equipment (which would increase the annual depreciation expense). Fixed expenses could decrease for the opposite reasons. But, we'll focus on the more likely situation—increases in fixed expenses.

Suppose total fixed expenses increase 10 percent due to general inflationary trends. There are no changes in the capacity of the business nor in the retail space or appearance of the space. As far as customers can tell, there have been no changes. Fixed expenses would increase 10 percent of $340,000, which is $34,000.

NEWCO could increase its sales price $34.00, with the additional $34,000 of fixed expenses spread over 1,000 units of sales. But this assumes that sales volume would remain the same at the higher price. Might not sales volume be decreased by the higher sales price? The $34 increase is not much, less than 2 percent. But sales volume might be sensitive to even such small increases. Many customers keep a sharp eye on prices.

To be safe, the business should allow for some decrease in sales volume. Indeed, this case closely parallels the previous situation in which a product cost increase is passed through to sales price. In that case the sales manager makes the conservative assumption that any percent increase in the sales price causes an equal percent decrease in sales volume. For example, if sales price goes up one percent (one point), then sales volume drops one percent (one point).

We'll make the same assumption here. Thus, the sales price would have to increase $47.00 to keep operating profit the same as the following Profit Profile shows (see Table 3–8). To be precise, sales price should be increased to $2,046.79, which is rounded to $2,047 in the Profit Profile.

The exact sales price was solved on a computer spreadsheet for the Profit Profile (I encourage you to try this approach if you know a spreadsheet program such as LOTUS 1–2–3). As before, the particular method of computation is not the main point here. Rather, managers should keep in mind that increasing sales price may decrease sales volume and should allow for this in their analysis.

TABLE 3–8
Profit Profile For 10% Fixed-Expenses Increase Offset By Decrease In Sales Volume

	Before	After	Change
Sales Volume	1,000 units	977 units	–23
Break-even Volume	680 units	684 units	4
Capacity Volume	1,250 units	1,250 units	0

	Per Unit		Total		
	Before	After	Before	After	Profit Impact
Sales Revenue	$ 2,000	$ 2,047	$ 2,000,000	$ 1,998,905	$ (1,095)
Product Cost	$(1,200)	$(1,200)	$(1,200,000)	$(1,171,924)	$ 28,076
Variable Expenses	$ (300)	$ (300)	$ (300,000)	$ (292,981)	$ 7,019
Profit Margin	$ 500	$ 547	$ 500,000	$ 534,000	$ 34,000
Fixed Expenses			$ (340,000)	$ (374,000)	$(34,000)
Operating Profit			$ 160,000	$ 160,000	$ 0

SUMMARY

Seldom does one primary profit factor change without changing at least one other factor. The joint, combined interaction effects of the changes should be carefully analyzed to make the best decision. Each situation is different.

If there is one key lesson, it is this. Keep your eye first and foremost on the *profit margin per unit*. Improvement in this key profit factor can overcome a large sales-volume drop, or almost any other negative change. By far, operating profit is most responsive to changes in the profit margin per unit, as several different situations in the chapter demonstrate.

There are only two basic ways to improve the profit margin per unit. Increase sales price. Or, decrease product cost and/or other variable expenses per unit. The sales price is the most external or visible part of the business, the factor most exposed to customer reaction. In contrast, product cost and variable expenses are more internal. Customers may not even be aware of these expense decreases unless such cost savings show through in lower product quality or worse service.

Last, the importance of protecting sales volume and market share has been mentioned several times in the chapter. Marketing managers certainly know what they're talking about on this point. Recovering lost market share is not easy, and could be fatal. Once gone, customers may never return.

CHAPTER 4

FINE-TUNING THE PROFIT PROFILE

A LOOK AHEAD

Ask a hundred business consultants and I'd bet all would say the first thing most new clients tell them is, "Our business is different." Which is true, of course; every business is unique. But at the same time, all businesses draw on a common core of concepts, principles, and techniques. Take people. Every individual is different and unique. Yet basic principles of behavior and motivation apply to all of us. Take products. Breakfast cereals are different from computers. Yet basic principles of marketing apply to both products.

Applying the basics is the really difficult part, which managers are paid to do and do well. The manager must adapt the broad concepts and general principles to the circumstances of the particular business. Likewise, the basic Profit Profiles used in previous chapters have to be adapted and modified to fit the characteristics of the particular business.

Two basic business examples have been used to lay the groundwork of basic analysis techniques that apply to all businesses. Being ignorant of these elementary analysis techniques would be comparable to the business manager being ignorant of the basic marketing concept of *positioning* a product, or being ignorant of the basic *financial* difference between debt and equity sources of capital. Although the Profit Profiles developed for the two basic examples are not perfect for every business, they provide the best starting point.

In this chapter we examine three major modifications of the basic business examples that have widespread relevance to many businesses:

- Some variable expenses are driven directly by sales *revenue,* such as sales commissions, credit card discounts, and bad debts from credit sales. To this point the business examples have included variable expenses based on sales *volume,* but not sales *revenue.* Sales-revenue-dependent expenses behave differently.
- Many businesses sell *services* instead of products. Indeed, the service sector accounts for a very large share of the American economy. The previous Profit Profiles are for product-oriented business. Service businesses do not have product costs, or have only minor product costs incidental to providing the service.
- Many businesses sell an extremely broad and diverse mix of products. There is *no common denominator* of sales volume. Thus, the sales-volume factor drops out of the Profit Profile, even though it has played such an important role to this point. Nevertheless, sales-price and sales-volume changes can be analyzed, if the sales mix of the business is held constant. New techniques are demonstrated for this situation.

Two other expenses are delayed to later chapters: *interest* and *income tax.* Interest is deductible for income tax and, thus, should be considered before income tax. However, interest depends on how the business is financed. A business could have no interest-bearing debt, or may be loaded with debt. Debt takes us over to the financial side of making profit where we examine the assets needed to conduct profit-making operations and the sources of capital for the assets. This broad area is covered in Part Two of this book. In this chapter, we stay with *operating profit,* which is profit before interest and income tax.

A FEW WORDS ABOUT PRODUCT COST

Product cost in the ice cream shop example in Chapters 1 and 2 is about 28 percent of sales revenue, which is fairly low compared with most businesses. In Chapter 3 NEWCO's product cost is 60 percent of sales price. Product cost varies greatly from industry to industry and from one broad product line to another.

For retail liquor stores product cost runs about 85 percent of sales revenue; for food supermarkets it's about 80 percent (although much lower on some products). For auto dealers product cost runs even higher; indeed, some of the ads you read suggest their product cost is 100 percent or more of sales revenue, which is not true. For other businesses, such as cosmetics and perfumes, product cost is surprisingly low. The fundamental analysis techniques explained in previous chapters are the same, whatever percent product cost happens to be.

Current product cost is the most relevant for decision making; managers are not anchored to past costs. In contrast, internal Profit Performance Reports to managers and external Income Statements to creditors and stockholders are prepared on the historical-cost basis. Decision making looks forward; profit accounting looks back.

During the last twelve months the product costs of a business may have increased (or decreased) two, three, or more times. These changes cause vexing problems in measuring and reporting profit. The key question is whether to follow a first-in, first-out cost-flow sequence, or conversely, to push the costs through in a last-in, first-out order. Both methods are acceptable to accountants, even though they lead to quite different profit measures.

For retailers and wholesalers product cost is their purchase cost; basically, product cost is invoice cost. In stark contrast, determining product cost is no easy matter for *manufacturers*. Product cost must be assembled from diverse types of production costs, some direct and some very indirect and far removed from the production line. Product costs of manufacturers are examined in the next chapter.

SALES-REVENUE-DEPENDENT EXPENSES

A New Profit Profile

Previous examples include variable expenses driven by sales volume. These expenses vary with the number of units sold, independent of the sales price of the units sold. Examples are packaging, delivery, and freight-out costs. Delivery and freight-out costs depend on the size and/or weight of the product, not sales value. For some businesses such costs might be quite material, for instance, General Motors delivering automobiles to its dealers all over the country. For other businesses these costs may be very small—the costs of bags for supermarkets, for example.

In contrast, many operating expenses vary with the *dollar amount* of sales revenue. Many retailers accept national credit cards, such as VISA, MasterCard, American Express, and Diners Club. The credit card charge slips are deposited daily with the local participating bank; the bank discounts the amount and credits the balance in the business' checking account. Discount rates vary between 3 to 6 percent (or higher). In short, the business nets only 97 to 94 cents on the dollar for credit card sales. The credit card discount expense comes right off the top of the sales dollar.

Another common example of sales-revenue-dependent expenses are sales commissions. As you know, many retailers and other businesses pay their sales representatives on a commission basis, which usually is a certain percent of the total sales amount

Many businesses extend short-term credit to their customers on open account, especially in selling to other businesses. No matter how carefully the seller screens customers before extending credit, a few never pay their debts to the business. Eventually, after making repeated collection efforts, the business ends up having to write off the receivable as uncollectible. These losses are called *bad debts* and are a normal expense of doing business on credit. Based on past experience, the business estimates what percent of total credit sales will end up as bad debts. This expense depends on the sales amount, not sales volume (number of units sold).

Another example of an expense that varies with sales revenue is one you might not suspect—rent. Businesses often sign lease agreements that call for rental amounts based on gross sales. There may be a base amount or fixed minimum monthly rent. In addition, there is a variable amount equal to a percent of total sales revenue. This is common for retailers renting space in shopping centers.

There are several other examples of expenses that vary with total sales revenue, such as franchise fees based on gross sales. In summary, the manager should identify all sales-revenue-dependent expenses and enter them as a key factor in the Profit Profile.

At this point, therefore, the Profit Profile is modified to include variable expenses driven by total sales revenue. The example for NEWCO is carried forward here, but modified to include the new variable-expense factor. We'll keep the sales-volume-variable-expense factor in the example to contrast the difference between the two types of variable expenses. See Table 4–1.

Notice the new factor in the Profit Profile—"Sales $ (Revenue Based) Expenses." The other variable expense factor is renamed "Sales Q (Quantity, or Volume Based) Expenses." Refer to the original example in Chapter 3 (see Table 3–1); notice that the old product cost of $1,200 is reduced to $1,000, and that the $200 difference is shifted to the new variable-expense factor in this modified example.

The Sales $ Expenses are 10 percent of total sales revenue. The $200 per unit means 10 percent of the sales price, *not* $200 per unit sold. If the sales price were lowered to $1,900 per unit, then these expenses would decrease to $190 per unit. The $200,000 total for these expenses is 10 percent of the $2,000,000 gross sales. If total sales revenue drops to $1,900,000, then the total of these variable expenses would be $190,000.

TABLE 4–1
NEWCO's Modified Profit Profile

Annual-Sales Volume	1,000 units	
Annual Break-even Volume	680 units	
Annual-Capacity Volume	1,250 units	
	Per Unit	*Total*
Sales Revenue	$ 2,000	$ 2,000,000
Sales $ Expenses	$ (200)	$ (200,000)
Product Cost	$(1,000)	$(1,000,000)
Sales Q Expenses	$ (300)	$ (300,000)
Profit Margin	$ 500	$ 500,000
Fixed Expenses		$ (340,000)
Operating Profit		$ 160,000

Ten Percent Sales-Price Decrease With Ten Percent Sales-Volume Increase—Still A Terrible Idea?

As before, suppose you're the sales manager. Since NEWCO is operating below its sales capacity, you are thinking of a 10 percent sales price cut. You predict sales volume would increase 10 percent. This is the same 10 percent trade-off plan examined in Chapter 3, but remember that the previous example does not include sales-revenue-based expenses. Comparisons are made between the two as we proceed.

Assuming you're correct about the sales-volume increase, what would happen to operating profit at the lower sales-price level? The comparative Profit Profile for this plan is shown in Table 4–2.

The sales price reduction is still a very poor idea given that sales volume increases only 10 percent; operating profit would decrease $148,000 to only $12,000. The sales-price-reduction plan would give away the farm—just about all the operating profit.

TABLE 4–2
Profit Profile for 10% Sales-Price Decrease & 10% Sales-Volume Increase

	Before		After		Changes
Sales Volume	1,000 units		1,100 units		100 units
Break-even Volume	680 units		1,063 units		383 units
Capacity Volume	1,250 units		1,250 units		
	Per Unit		Total		
	Before	After	Before	After	Profit Impact
Sales Revenue	$ 2,000	$ 1,800	$ 2,000,000	$ 1,980,000	$ (20,000)
Sales $ Expenses	$ (200)	$ (180)	$ (200,000)	$ (198,000)	$ 2,000
Product Cost	$(1,000)	$(1,000)	$(1,000,000)	$(1,100,000)	$(100,000)
Sales Q Expenses	$ (300)	$ (300)	$ (300,000)	$ (330,000)	$ (30,000)
Profit Margin	$ 500	$ 320	$ 500,000	$ 352,000	$(148,000)
Fixed Expenses			$ (340,000)	$ (340,000)	
Operating Profit			$ 160,000	$ 12,000	$(148,000)

The only good thing that can be said is that this situation isn't quite as bad as the one before. In the previous case the 10 percent sales-price/sales-volume trade-off was even worse. Operating profit dropped $170,000 in that situation to cause a loss of $10,000. In this case the business would still be above its break-even volume, though just barely.

Notice the sales-revenue-dependent expenses in this situation. These expenses *decrease* $2,000, which is 10 percent of the decrease in sales revenue. When cutting sales prices it's better to have expenses that go down with sales revenue than expenses that go up with sales volume.

Ten Percent Sales-Price Increase With Ten Percent Sales-Volume Decrease—Still Too Good To Be True?

Would it be a good idea to increase sales prices 10 percent even if sales volume were to drop 10 percent? Table 4–3 shows what would happen.

TABLE 4–3
Profit Profile for 10% Sales-Price Increase & 10% Sales-Volume Decrease

	Before	After	Changes
Sales Volume	1,000 units	900 units	−100 units
Break-even Volume	680 units	500 units	−180 units
Capacity Volume	1,250 units	1,250 units	

	Per Unit		Total		Profit Impact
	Before	After	Before	After	
Sales Revenue	$ 2,000	$ 2,200	$ 2,000,000	$1,980,000	$ (20,000)
Sales $ Expenses	$ (200)	$ (220)	$ (200,000)	$ (198,000)	$ 2,000
Product Cost	$(1,000)	$(1,000)	$(1,000,000)	$ (900,000)	$100,000
Sales Q Expenses	$ (300)	$ (300)	$ (300,000)	$ (270,000)	$ 30,000
Profit Margin	$ 500	$ 680	$ 500,000	$ 612,000	$112,000
Fixed Expenses			$ (340,000)	$ (340,000)	
Operating Profit			$ 160,000	$ 272,000	$112,000

Operating profit increases nicely to $272,000. The break-even point drops to 500 units because the profit margin per unit increases to $680. In Chapter 3 operating profit increases even more to $290,000, and the break-even point is even lower.

The earlier warning should be repeated here. Sales managers are leery of giving up sales volume, especially if it means a smaller market share. Any sales-volume decrease is not taken lightly. The long-term ability of the business to compete requires a strong sales base. The increase in operating profit may not continue very long if the smaller sales volume were to undercut the long-term marketing strengths and advantages of the business.

SERVICE BUSINESSES

Building The Basic Profit Profile

A broad definition for service-based businesses would range from dry cleaners to film processors, from hotels to hospitals, from airlines to freight haulers, from CPAs to barbers, from rental firms to photo copying stores, and so forth. Without a doubt, the service sector is one of the biggest in the economy, but extremely diverse. Service businesses, including personal and professional service firms, span a very broad spectrum.

The purpose here is to present a basic Profit Profile that's a useful analysis framework for most service-oriented businesses. This basic example can be easily modified to fit the characteristics of a particular service business. Our business is called SERVECO.

If you think about it, in many cases an incidental product is sold with the service. For example, a copying business such as Kinko's Copies sells paper to its customers. Of course, the main thing sold is the copying service, not the paper. Airlines sell transportation, but they also provide food and beverages in flight. Hotels are not really in the business of selling towels, but they know that many guests take towels with them on the way out.

True, many personal and professional service firms sell no product at all, such as architect and CPA firms. And some service businesses do not either. However, a small product cost is included in the basic example. This is more common than no product cost at all. The product cost can be easily removed if it doesn't apply. For analysis purposes it's better to keep it in the example. The more difficult question concerns other variable expenses.

Many service businesses have expenses that vary with total sales *revenue*. Credit card discounts, sales commissions, and franchise fees come to mind again. Many service businesses also have expenses that vary with sales *volume* (the number of passengers flown by an airline, or the number of hotel guests, for instance). Sales-revenue-based expenses are more important for most service businesses and are included in the Profit Profile for SERVECO. Sales-volume-dependent expenses are not included. (Recall that a minor product cost is included, which varies with sales volume.)

Most service businesses are saddled with large fixed expenses. Service takes people, so most service businesses have a large number of employees who are paid fixed salaries or hourly rates based on the standard forty-hour work week. Many service businesses, such as movie theaters and airlines, have large investments in buildings and/or equipment. A fixed amount of depreciation expense is recorded each year. Many other fixed expenses could be listed. In sum, the example includes a large fixed-expenses factor.

The Profit Profile for SERVECO is shown in Table 4-4.

Notice right away that sales volume is expressed *not* as a number of units, but instead, as a *percent of capacity*. Examples are the occupancy rate for a hotel, or the passenger load factor for an airline. Many service businesses sell a variety of services, such as first-class-versus-coach seats by an airline, or single versus double rooms by a hotel. Instead of separating every different type of service, a broader measure of sales activity is more useful for decision analysis. This example uses percent of capacity to illustrate a different concept and way of measuring sales volume.

Variable expenses are driven by total sales *revenue;* these expenses are 15 percent of gross sales. In contrast, product cost is driven by sales *volume*. As just explained, sales volume is not stated in number of units, but rather in *percentage points* of sales

TABLE 4–4
Profit Profile For SERVECO

Sales Volume as % of Capacity	80%
Sales Revenue	$1,000,000
Variable Expenses	$ (150,000)
Product Cost	$ (50,000)
Profit Margin	$ 800,000
Fixed Expenses	$ (650,000)
Operating Profit	$ 150,000

capacity. In other words, one point of sales capacity is the basic unit of sales activity at the overall analysis level.

Presently the business is operating at an overall sales volume equal to 80 points of sales capacity. Product cost depends on sales volume, so each point of sales activity carries a product cost of $625:

$50,000 product cost/80 points = $625 per point

Notice that fixed expenses are fairly high compared with total sales revenue, which as just mentioned is typical for service businesses. Even so, the business makes operating profit of $150,000 which seems fairly good. Keep in mind, however, that this amount is before interest and income tax are deducted. Also, there might be year-end management bonuses not yet deducted from the operating profit of $150,000.

Getting Started: Computing The Break-even Point

You may have noticed that the break-even point is not given in the Profit Profile, which is deliberate. We now determine the break-even point. To repeat: Sales volume is expressed in points of capacity. Each point produces $12,500 sales revenue:

$1,000,000 Sales Revenue/80 points = $12,500

Variable expenses "take away" 15 percent of this amount or $1,875 per point:

$12,500 Sales Revenue × 15% = $1,875

So, the net sales revenue is $10,625 per point:

$12,500 Sales Revenue − $1,875 Variable Expense = $10,625

Product cost is $625 per point, as already computed. So, each point of sales activity contributes $10,000 towards covering fixed expenses:

$10,625 net sales revenue − $625 product cost = $10,000

Notice in the Profit Profile that total profit margin is $800,000, which is the $10,000 per point just computed times 80 points of sales volume.

Total fixed expenses are $650,000. Since the profit margin is $10,000 per point, it takes 65 points to break even. The business must operate at 65 percent sales capacity to break even, as shown in Table 4–5.

As you can see, sales would have to decrease to $812,500 from the present level of $1,000,000 before the company would drop to a zero operating profit—assuming there is no reduction in its fixed expenses at the lower sales level. If the business could forecast such a large fall-off in sales revenue, it probably would have to lay off some employees or take other steps to reduce its fixed expenses.

Ten Percent Changes—A Big Deal

What's the operating profit impact of 10 percent changes in sales price and sales volume for the service business? Table 4–6 com-

TABLE 4–5
SERVECO's Break-even Profit Profile

Sales Volume as % of Capacity	65%
Sales Revenue	$ 812,500
Variable Expenses	$(121,875)
Product Cost	$ (40,625)
Profit Margin	$ 650,000
Fixed Expenses	$(650,000)
Operating Profit	$ 0

TABLE 4–6
Ten Percent Sales-Price Changes

	Present	Increase 10%	Decrease 10%
Sales Revenue	$ 12,500.00	$ 13,750.00	$ 11,250.00
Variable Expenses	$ (1,875.00)	$ (2,062.50)	$ (1,687.50)
Product Cost	$ (625.00)	$ (625.00)	$ (625.00)
Profit Margin	$ 10,000.00	$ 11,062.50	$ 8,937.50
Sales Volume In Points	80	80	80
Total Profit Margin	$ 800,000.00	$ 885,000.00	$ 715,000.00
Total Fixed Expenses	$(650,000.00)	$(650,000.00)	$(650,000.00)
Operating Profit	$ 150,000.00	$ 235,000.00	$ 65,000.00

pares operating profit results for both a 10 percent sales-price increase and decrease for the service business example. As you can see, operating profit changes ± $85,000, which is a very large 57 percent swing in profit.

In previous examples for product businesses a 10 percent sales-price change has a much bigger impact on profit than a 10 percent sales-volume change. Would the same be true for a service business? Table 4–7 shows operating profit results for 10 percent sales-volume changes for SERVECO.

A 10 percent sales-volume change causes almost as much swing in operating profit as the 10 percent sales-price change. The sales-price changes are only $5,000 better or worse compared with the sales-volume changes—not much difference. This is in sharp contrast to product businesses where sales-price changes cause much larger operating-profit swings than sales-volume changes.

A 10 percent sales-price change causes SERVECO's profit margin per point to change about the same percent. In fact, it would be exactly 10 percent except for the small product cost that remains the same per point of capacity. In contrast, look again at one of the product business examples, say the earlier one in this Chapter (see Table 4–1). Profit margin per unit is $500 compared with a sales price of $2,000, or only one fourth of the sales price. A 10 percent sales price shift in that example changes profit margin by $180, which is a 36 percent change in this key factor.

TABLE 4–7
Ten Percent Sales-Volume Changes

	Present	Increase 10%	Decrease 10%
Sales Revenue	$ 12,500.00	$ 12,500.00	$ 12,500.00
Variable Expenses	$ (1,875.00)	$ (1,875.00)	$ (1,875.00)
Product Cost	$ (625.00)	$ (625.00)	$ (625.00)
Profit Margin	$ 10,000.00	$ 10,000.00	$ 10,000.00
Sales Volume In Points	80	88	72
Total Profit Margin	$ 800,000.00	$ 880,000.00	$ 720,000.00
Total Fixed Expenses	$(650,000.00)	$(650,000.00)	$ (650,000.00)
Operating Profit	$ 150,000.00	$ 230,000.00	$ 70,000.00

The percent of sales-price change is, in fact, *not* what managers should focus on. *What percent does profit margin change?* This is the key question. For service businesses, who have little or no product cost, a 10 percent sales-price change causes about an equal percent change in profit margin. But, for product businesses, a 10 percent sales price change causes a 20, 30, or 40 percent change in profit margin. This basic difference between the two types of businesses is extremely important in trade-off decisions.

Trade-Off Decisions—No Big Deal

Suppose you are considering a 10 percent sales-price decrease. You predict sales volume would increase 10 percent. We have already analyzed this trade-off for product businesses; the result is a very large *decrease* in operating profit. Would the same be true for a service business? The comparative Profit Profile for SERVECO is shown in Table 4–8.

Operating profit decreases, though only slightly, and nothing on the scale of the large decreases in previous examples for product businesses. The main reason for the much smaller decrease in operating profit is that product cost for a service business is very low, perhaps even zero. Thus, an increase in sales volume does not increase total product cost very much. Look in Table 4–8 again if you would; the $10,000 sales revenue de-

TABLE 4-8
SERVECO's Profit Profile
For 10% Sales-Price Decrease & 10% Sales-Volume Increase

	Before	After	Changes
Sales Volume as % of Capacity	80%	88%	
Sales Revenue	$1,000,000	$ 990,000	$(10,000)
Variable Expenses	$ (150,000)	$(148,500)	$ 1,500
Product Cost	$ (50,000)	$ (55,000)	$ (5,000)
Profit Margin	$ 800,000	$ 786,500	$(13,500)
Fixed Expenses	$ (650,000)	$(650,000)	
Operating Profit	$ 150,000	$ 136,500	$(13,500)

crease is the major reason for the operating-profit decrease. The product-cost increase is only $5,000 in this example.

What about the opposite 10 percent trade-off? Suppose sales price is increased 10 percent with a 10 percent decrease in sales volume. The comparative Profit Profile is shown in Table 4-9.

Notice that SERVECO's operating profit would decrease $3,500. For product businesses, this trade-off *increases* operating profit by a large percent. If you recall, for product companies the gain in operating profit is due primarily to product cost savings at the lower sales volume. For service businesses, product-cost savings are quite small at the lower sales level. Most of the "action" is with sales revenue, which decreases $10,000. If a service business had no product cost at all, then all the action is in the sales revenue and the corresponding changes in variable expenses based on sales revenue.

NO COMMON DENOMINATOR OF SALES VOLUME?

Many businesses have a very diverse sales mix. They sell hundreds or thousands of different products, to say nothing of different sizes and different brands of the same product. For instance, supermarkets sell a huge variety of food products as well as books, magazines, flowers, and so on. The number of breakfast cereal boxes sold can't be added to number of heads of lettuce, or number of magazines, or pounds of hamburger, and

TABLE 4-9
SERVECO's Profit Profile For
10% Sales-Price Increase & 10% Sales-Volume Decrease

	Before	After	Changes
Sales Volume as % of Capacity	80%	72%	
Sales Revenue	$1,000,000	$ 990,000	$(10,000)
Variable Expenses	$ (150,000)	$(148,500)	$ 1,500
Product Cost	$ (50,000)	$ (45,000)	$ 5,000
Profit Margin	$ 800,000	$ 796,500	$ (3,500)
Fixed Expenses	$ (650,000)	$(650,000)	
Operating Profit	$ 150,000	$ 146,500	$ (3,500)

so on. There is *no common denominator of sales volume*—other than sales dollars.

So it would seem that the sales-volume factor drops out for any sort of aggregate analysis for the business as a whole, or for any analysis that goes beyond one defined product line. Well, this isn't quite true.

Suppose DIVERSECO sells a very broad range of different products, such as the supermarket just mentioned or a large hardware/variety store that sells everything from light bulbs, tools, TVs, clothing, etc. The company president, who takes the total company-wide view of things, has summarized results for last year in Table 4-10 for the business as a whole. (The president must have read this book.)

No sales-volume factor is given, because the company has a very diversified sales mix. (The company sells mainly products, although we could just as well assume that some services are

Table 4-10
Profit Profile For DIVERSECO

Sales Revenue	$10,000,000
Product Cost	$ (6,000,000)
Expenses	$ (1,000,000)
Profit Margin	$ 3,000,000
Fixed Expenses	$ (2,000,000)
Operating Profit	$ 1,000,000

included.) Some products have higher profit margins than others, so a change in the sales mix would change the ratio of total product cost to total sales revenue. In the following analysis sales mix is held constant. (Sales mix changes are discussed in a later chapter.)

The president would like to know the effects of a 10 percent across-the-board-sales-price reduction if there were a 10 percent sales-volume increase across the board on all items sold. There is no common denominator of sales volume, but this doesn't prevent the analysis of the president's plan. However, it does force us to get more specific about variable expenses.

Are the variable expenses primarily sales-revenue or sales-volume dependent? This key question must be answered before the analysis can be done. The president says there are predominantly sales-revenue-based expenses, such as credit card discount expense and sales commissions. Customers carry out everything bought, so there are no delivery expenses or any other expenses dependent on sales volume.

Aggregate level analysis is shown in the following schedule, which uses a two-step approach (see Table 4–11). First the sales-price effect by itself is computed, and then the sales-volume effect is computed on top of the sales-price effect.

The 10 percent sales-price decrease by itself, and before considering the sales-volume increase, changes only two factors—sales revenue and variable expenses. See the sales-price-step column.

Second, the 10 percent volume increase is taken into account, building on the changes caused by the sales-price de-

TABLE 4–11
DIVERSECO—10% Sales-Price Decrease & 10% Sales-Volume Increase

	Present	Sales Price Step	Sales Volume Step	Changes
Sales Revenue	$10,000,000	$9,000,000	$ 9,900,000	$(100,000)
Product Cost	$ (6,000,000)		$(6,600,000)	$(600,000)
Variable Expenses	$ (1,000,000)	$ (900,000)	$ (990,000)	$ 10,000
Profit Margin	$ 3,000,000		$ 2,310,000	$(690,000)
Fixed Expenses	$ (2,000,000)		$(2,000,000)	
Operating Profit	$ 1,000,000		$ 310,000	$(690,000)

crease. The $9,000,000 sales revenue figure (which gives effect to the 10 percent sales-price reduction) is "scaled up" to reflect the 10 percent volume increase. Product cost increases 10 percent which obviously depends on sales volume. Variable expenses also increase 10 percent from the $900,000 figure. Thus, profit margin drops to $2,310,000 for a $690,000 decrease.

Fixed costs remain the same, which assumes that the business has enough idle capacity to absorb the sales-volume increase without having to increase any of these expenses. This might not be the case. We would have to ask the president about this. Could a 10 percent sales-volume increase be handled by the present number of employees, the present retail and backroom storage space of the store, and the present equipment? If not, the president would have to estimate how much fixed expenses would increase to provide the additional sales-volume capacity. We'll assume enough slack to permit a 10 percent sales-volume increase, so fixed expenses remain the same.

Therefore, this trade-off would be a disaster; operating profit would plunge to $310,000, a 69 percent drop. The sales-price reduction on all items is too steep given that sales-volume increases only 10 percent. The reasons are much the same as explained in previous examples; sales revenue decreases a little and product cost increases a lot.

The president also asks what would happen for the reverse trade-off—a 10 percent sales-price increase that causes a 10 percent sales-volume decrease. Table 4–12 shows the two-step analysis of this plan.

TABLE 4–12
DIVERSECO—10% Sales-Price Increase & 10% Sales-Volume Decrease

	Present	Sales-Price Step	Sales-Volume Step	Changes
Sales Revenue	$10,000,000	$11,000,000	$ 9,900,000	$(100,000)
Product Cost	$ (6,000,000)		$(5,400,000)	$ 600,000
Variable Expenses	$ (1,000,000)	$ (1,100,000)	$ (990,000)	$ 10,000
Profit Margin	$ 3,000,000		$ 3,510,000	$ 510,000
Fixed Expenses	$ (2,000,000)		$(2,000,000)	
Operating Profit	$ 1,000,000		$ 1,510,000	$ 510,000

As you may have anticipated, operating profit increases substantially. Of course, sales volume may drop more than 10 percent. (Sales volume would have to drop more than 23 percent to cause operating profit to decrease.) The more intriguing question is whether the president would give up sales volume to make more operating profit. Would you?

SUMMARY

Many businesses have sizable amounts of variable expenses that depend on sales revenue instead of or in addition to those that depend on sales volume. Accordingly, the business example is modified to include this new factor. Though necessary to portray these companies realistically, the modification does not make all that much difference compared with a similar product-oriented business that does not have any sales-revenue-dependent expenses. Basically, operating profit changes caused by sales-price/sales-volume trade-offs are dampened down a little, but the main effects are still largely the same.

Service businesses, having no product cost or only minimal product cost incidental to selling the service, are quite another story. Most of these companies have sizable variable expenses and very large fixed expenses. Sales-price changes have a very big impact on operating profit; so do sales-volume changes. In fact, there's not much difference between the two. An equal sales price/sales-volume trade-off has very little impact on operating profit for a service business, which is in sharp contrast to product businesses.

Diversified businesses that sell many different product lines have no common denominator of sales volume. Nevertheless, aggregate-level analysis is possible, if sales mix is held constant. The two-step analysis—in which the sales-price change is computed first and then the sales-volume change is added on—is a very handy technique to determine quickly changes in the Profit Profile for the business.

CHAPTER 5

PRODUCT COST OF MANUFACTURERS

Managers of manufacturing businesses should know how product cost is determined, not the detailed cost accounting procedures, but rather the basic methods of determining product cost per unit. Product cost is a *composite* number, consisting of materials, labor, and overhead costs. Each component is subject to different dynamics and presents different management problems.

This chapter is a quick overview of the basic methods and problems of determining product cost for the manufacturing business. Technical cost-accounting procedures and issues are avoided. But this doesn't mean the manager should know nothing about manufacturing-cost accounting. The worst thing a manager can do is to take the product cost supplied by the accountant and simply plug this number into a Profit Profile.

The chapter examines four key management questions about product cost of manufacturers:

1. Where does the accumulation of *product* cost stop? In other words, which costs are manufacturing versus other, non-manufacturing costs of operating the business?
2. Should product cost be based on the *production capacity* available during the period or the *actual output* during the period?
3. How should manufacturing *inefficiency* be handled in determination of product cost? Ideally there should be no inefficiency, but as a practical matter usually there is some inefficiency.

4. If *too many units* are produced, should the excess ending inventory be carried at full-product cost?

MANUFACTURERS VERSUS RETAILERS (AND WHOLESALERS)

Retailers and wholesalers buy products in finished condition ready for resale. They buy products from manufacturers who are the producers, the original sources of products. In classical economic terms, manufacturers add *form* utility (value) to products. Wholesalers and retailers, being channels of distribution, add *time*-and-*place* utility to products.

Product cost is basically purchase cost for retailers and wholesalers. Determining product cost is much different for manufacturers. The manufacturing process may be simple and short or complex and long. It may be labor intensive or capital (asset) intensive. Products may roll off a continuous mass-production assembly line, such as boxes of breakfast cereal. Or production may be discontinuous and done on a "job order" basis, such as printing and binding 10,000 copies of one book and then starting over on the next book.

The range and variety of manufacturing in the American economy is truly amazing. Look down a list of manufacturers, such as the annual *Fortune 500 Industrials* ranking. You'll find a very wide diversity of products and manufacturing processes. Nevertheless, all manufacturers use certain basic methods in determining product cost, and all face more or less the same problems.

The example in this chapter is an established manufacturing business, one that has been operating many years. Its managers have already assembled and organized machines, equipment, tools, and employees into a smooth running production process that is dependable and efficient—a monumental task, to say the least. Plant location is critical, as is plant layout, employee training, materials procurement, complying with an ever-broadening range of governmental regulations, and so on. These points are only mentioned in passing in order to move on to product-cost determination.

THE CRUX OF PRODUCT COST: MANUFACTURING COSTS DIVIDED BY PRODUCTION OUTPUT

Many manufacturers determine product cost monthly, others quarterly. There is no one standard period; it could be done weekly, or even daily. In any case, the length of the time period is not crucial to the basic concepts and methods of determining product cost. Many fixed manufacturing costs are one-year commitments. Also, the year is a natural time period for management planning and financial reporting. Thus, the year is the time period for our example.

A business called MANUFACTCO manufactures one product in its one production plant. For the year just ended its Manufacturing Cost Profile is presented in Table 5–1.

Raw materials are purchased parts and materials that become part of the product. Direct labor refers to those employees who work on the production line. Direct labor costs should include fringe benefits which can add 30–40 percent or more to basic wage rates. Manufacturing overhead refers to everything else. Some of these costs vary with total output, such as electricity that powers the machinery. But most overhead costs are fixed over the short run and do not depend on the level of production activity, such as property taxes and fire insurance on the production plant.

Fixed manufacturing overhead costs provide *production capacity* for the period. MANUFACTCO's annual production capacity is 12,000 units. Its $2,100,000 total fixed overhead costs provide the facilities and people to produce this many units under normal, practical conditions of operation. Notice that pro-

TABLE 5–1
Manufacturing-Cost Profile

Practical-Production Capacity		12,000 units
Actual Output During Period		12,000 units
	Total	Per Unit
Raw-Materials Costs	$2,580,000	$215.00
Direct-Labor Costs	$3,120,000	$260.00
Variable-Overhead Costs	$ 420,000	$ 35.00
Fixed-Overhead Costs	$2,100,000	$175.00
Total Manufacturing Costs	$8,220,000	$685.00

duction output for the year equals capacity. Actual output usually falls short of capacity; we will look at this problem later.

The crux of determining product cost is dividing manufacturing cost by production output, which is shown for each cost component in the Manufacturing Cost Profile. To sum up, the fundamental concept of product cost is seen in the following computation:

$$\text{Total Manufacturing Costs/Total Output} \\ = \text{Product Cost Per Unit} \\ \$8{,}220{,}000/12{,}000 \text{ units} = \$685.00$$

Notice immediately three things about product cost per unit. First, product cost is a *calculated* amount. It doesn't exist until it's computed; the computation is everything. Clearly, both the numerator and the denominator of the computation must be correct, or else the product cost per unit is wrong.

Second, product cost is an *average* amount. Total cost for a period of time is divided by total output over that same period, which is one year in this example. Costs and quantities may vary daily, weekly, or monthly, but the essential definition and computation of product cost per unit is the average for a certain period of time.

Third, *only manufacturing costs* are included. All production costs should be included, but no other business operating expenses. This third point is extraordinarily important.

PRODUCT VERSUS PERIOD COSTS

A clear line must be drawn between manufacturing costs and all other costs of operating the business. A manufacturer must separate between these two types of costs. This classification is the absolute first step. Product (manufacturing) cost is accumulated in an inventory account and held in this asset account until products are sold.[1] Cost-of-goods-sold expense is not re-

---

[1] During production, manufacturing costs are first accumulated in an inventory account called Work-In-Process; when production is completed, the cost of completed units is transferred to the Finished-Goods-Inventory account.

corded until products are sold, i.e., not until there is sales revenue against which the product cost is deducted.

In contrast, non-manufacturing costs are charged against sales revenue in the period these costs are recorded. For this reason, non-manufacturing costs are called *period* costs. None of these costs are put into an inventory account. They go immediately into an expense account. (Some, such as insurance premiums covering several months, spend time in the Prepaid Expenses account before being charged off as an expense.) Sales and marketing costs, such as advertising, are not included in product cost; these are viewed as costs of making sales, not making products. Research and development costs are not classified as product costs either, even though R&D costs may lead to new products, or new methods of manufacture, or new compounds of materials, or other kinds of technological improvements.

Raw materials and direct labor costs are no problem; clearly these are manufacturing costs. Direct materials and labor are easily matched with particular products being manufactured. Variable overhead, in contrast, presents problems of matching with particular products, and fixed overhead is a real headache. Overhead means *indirect,* or removed from the production line; thus, there is no obvious basis of association with particular products.

Consider, for example, the manufacture of 10,000 copies of a book. The paper-and-ink cost (raw materials) can be identified to each production run. Likewise, the employees setting up and operating the presses (direct labor) can be identified. Variable overhead cannot be directly identified with particular press runs; instead, it must be allocated. For instance, the cost of electricity to power the presses can be allocated on the basis of the machine hours of each run.

Much more troublesome are fixed overhead costs, such as the annual property taxes on the production plant, depreciation of the printing presses, the fixed salary of the plant nurse, the fixed salary of the vice president of production, and so on. Fixed manufacturing overhead costs have to be allocated among different products based on some common denominator of production activity. The fixed overhead cost allocation problem is discussed later in the chapter. MANUFACTCO makes only one product, so all costs are matched with this one product.

The first requirement is to separate cleanly between manufacturing overhead costs and other operating costs of the business. A line of demarcation must be drawn. The 1986 Tax Reform Act (TRA) takes a special interest in this problem, probably because many manufacturers were careless in classifying between manufacturing overhead and non-manufacturing operating costs. The general rules of the '86 TRA are discussed in a recent article.[2] The relevant schedule from this article is reproduced on the next page (see Table 5–2).

"Capitalize" means to record the cost as a product cost, i.e., to classify the cost as manufacturing overhead that is allocated to products. In other words, capitalized costs are put in an inventory-asset account and held in the account as a capital investment until the products are sold.

We won't go into all the details. The main point is that managers should definitely know which specific costs are classified as product costs and which are expensed. As the article points out, marketing and distribution costs and research and development costs are *not* classified as product costs. In the Profit Profile these costs would be either a variable or fixed operating expense.

IMPACT OF CLASSIFICATION ERRORS ON OPERATING PROFIT

MANUFACTCO sold 11,000 units during the year just ended. It manufactured 12,000 units during the year, so inventory increased 1,000 units. MANUFACTCO's Profit Profile for the year and its supporting Manufacturing Cost Profile are presented in Table 5–3.

Notice that only $7,535,000 total product cost is deducted as Cost-of-Goods-Sold Expense from sales revenue.[3] You may ask what happens to the $685,000 difference between the $8,220,000 total manufacturing costs for the year and the $7,535,000 de-

---

[2]Jose A. Rullan and Robert S. Landman, "Coping with the New Inventory Capitalization Rules," *Journal of Accountancy,* January 1988, pp. 110–116.

[3]Depending on which inventory method the business uses—LIFO or FIFO—the total cost-of-goods-sold expense for the year might be somewhat different.

TABLE 5-2
Inventory capitalization requirements

Costs	Pre-TRA	Post-TRA
Manufacturers:		
Category 1 costs:		
Repairs and maintenance	Capitalize	Capitalize
Occupancy costs	Capitalize	Capitalize
Indirect labor	Capitalize	Capitalize
Production supervision	Capitalize	Capitalize
Indirect materials and supplies	Capitalize	Capitalize
Miscellaneous tools	Capitalize	Capitalize
Quality control	Capitalize	Capitalize
Category 2 costs:		
Marketing and distribution	Expense	Expense
Interest not related to the production process	Expense	Expense
Research and development	Expense	Expense
Product development costs	Expense	Capitalize
Percent depletion in excess of cost	Expense	Capitalize
Excess depreciation	Expense	Capitalize
Income taxes	Expense	Expense
Past service pension cost	Expense	Expense
General and administrative, if benefiting production	Expense	Capitalize
Officers' salaries, if benefiting production	Expense	Capitalize
Category 3 costs:		
Taxes (other than income) relate to production assets	Optional	Capitalize
Depreciation and depletion	Optional	Capitalize
Employee benefits (production)	Optional	Capitalize
Cost of strikes	Optional	Expense
Rework, scrap, spoilage	Optional	Capitalize

ducted as expense. The $685,000 goes into inventory; 1,000 units were produced in excess of the units sold which at $685.00 each equals $685,000. The inventory-asset account increases $685,000.

Suppose you're the General Manager, and you just discovered that the business misclassified some of its fixed costs. Fixed manufacturing overhead costs should have been $480,000 more; these costs were erroneously classified as fixed operating expenses. You ask for revised reports that correct the error. The revised Profit Profile and Manufacturing Cost Profile are shown in Table 5-4.

TABLE 5-3

MANUFACTCO's Profit Profile

Sales Volume For Year		11,000 units
	Per Unit	Total
Sales Revenue	$1,400.00	$15,400,000
Product Cost	$ (685.00)	$ (7,535,000)
Variable-Operating Expenses	$ (305.00)	$ (3,355,000)
Profit Margin	$ 410.00	$ 4,510,000
Fixed-Operating Expenses		$ (2,300,000)
Operating Profit		$ 2,210,000

MANUFACTO'S Manufacturing Cost Profile

Practical-Production Capacity		12,000 units
Actual Output During Period		12,000 units
	Total	Per Unit
Raw-Materials Costs	$2,580,000	$215.00
Direct-Labor Costs	$3,120,000	$260.00
Variable-Overhead Costs	$ 420,000	$ 35.00
Fixed-Overhead Costs	$2,100,000	$175.00
Total Manufacturing Costs	$8,220,000	$685.00

Fixed operating expenses are reduced $480,000 (from $2,300,000 to $1,820,000); this amount is shifted to fixed manufacturing overhead costs which increases from $2,100,000 to $2,580,000. Thus $480,000 additional fixed overhead is "loaded" on the 12,000 units produced, which increases product cost $40 per unit (from $685 to $725).

Notice that 1,000 of the 12,000 units manufactured went into ending inventory, not out the door to customers. Each of the 1,000 units carries $40.00 more fixed overhead cost for a total of $40,000 additional cost in ending inventory. This additional $40,000 is not charged to Cost-of-Goods-Sold Expense, which is only $440,000 higher than before (from $7,535,000 to $7,975,000). Thus, revised Operating Profit is $40,000 higher than before. In one sense, we have "manufactured" $40,000 more operating profit simply by reclassifying costs from operating to manufacturing.

TABLE 5–4

MANUFACTCO's Profit Profile

Sales Volume For Year   11,000 units

	Before		Revised	
	Per Unit	Total	Per Unit	Total
Sales Revenue	$1,400.00	$15,400,000	$1,400.00	$15,400,000
Product Cost	$ (685.00)	$ (7,535,000)	$ (725.00)	$ (7,975,000)
Variable-Operating Expenses	$ (305.00)	$ (3,355,000)	$ (305.00)	$ (3,355,000)
Profit Margin	$ 410.00	$ 4,510,000	$ 370.00	$ 4,070,000
Fixed-Operating Expenses		$ (2,300,000)		$ (1,820,000)
Operating Profit		$ 2,210,000		$ 2,250,000

MANUFACTO's Manufacturing-Cost Profile

Practical-Production Capacity   12,000 units
Actual Output During Period   12,000 units

	Before		Revised	
	Total	Per Unit	Total	Per Unit
Raw-Materials Costs	$2,580,000	$215.00	$2,580,000	$215.00
Direct-Labor Costs	$3,120,000	$260.00	$3,120,000	$260.00
Variable-Overhead Costs	$ 420,000	$ 35.00	$ 420,000	$ 35.00
Fixed-Overhead Costs	$2,100,000	$175.00	$2,580,000	$215.00
Total Manufacturing Costs	$8,220,000	$685.00	$8,700,000	$725.00

This situation illustrates the importance of proper classification of costs. Classification errors can be in either direction; too much cost could be put into manufacturing. However, most often businesses don't put enough costs into manufacturing. Costs that should be included in manufacturing are deliberately put into the non-manufacturing (operating expenses) category, which minimizes product cost. The '86 Tax Reform Act clearly attempts to deal with this abuse.

In any case, managers should keep alert. When setting sales price based on mark-up percentages, managers should have a clear understanding of whether all overhead costs are included in product cost. Operating profit is typically a major factor in evaluating management performance. In fact, the manager's annual bonus may depend on operating profit. Clearly, managers should know the impact of cost classification is on product cost and operating profit.

IDLE-PRODUCTION CAPACITY

Most manufacturers have very large fixed manufacturing overhead costs, including depreciation of plant and equipment, salaries of a wide range of employees (from the Vice President of Production to janitors), fire insurance costs, property taxes, and so on. Variable manufacturing costs (raw materials, direct labor, and variable overhead) depend on the quantity produced. No output, no variable costs. Double output and variable costs double. In contrast, fixed overhead costs remain relatively flat over a broad range of production levels.

More importantly, fixed manufacturing overhead costs provide *production capacity*. Every fixed cost can be traced back to an essential factor of production that is needed in the manufacturing process: buildings, machinery, equipment, tools, the work force, and so on. A building is bought and then depreciated over many years; annual depreciation is a fixed cost. Even if the building is leased, the monthly rent is a fixed cost that does not depend on the number of units produced during the month. Likewise for machinery, equipment, and tools. Managers should measure the production capacity provided by their fixed manufacturing overhead costs. Capacity is a key measure of course; it's the maximum production output during a period of time from the facilities in place and ready for use. Fixed overhead costs are the irreducible amount the facilities cost over the short-term.

Suppose MANUFACTCO's annual production capacity, given its $2,100,000 total annual fixed manufacturing overhead costs, is 15,000 units. (Earlier a lower capacity is assumed equal to the production output of the period.) Assume the business correctly classifies its costs between manufacturing and operating;

we've already discussed the importance of this basic classification of costs.

The company manufactured 12,000 units during the year; idle capacity is 3,000 units, i.e., its unused production capacity. Fixed manufacturing overhead costs would have been no more if 15,000 units had been manufactured, or for that matter, would have been no less if fewer units had been produced. In short, the company operated at 80 percent of capacity (12,000/15,000 units = 80%). It should be pointed out that 20 percent idle capacity is not that unusual. For example, an Associated Press report for January 1988 states:

> The nation's industrial operating rate was unchanged in January at 82.2 percent of capacity. ... Manufacturers of durable goods ... operated at 79.9 percent of capacity ... while manufacturers of non-durable goods operated at 86.1 percent of capacity. Normally, when operating rates get about 85 percent, economists begin to worry about bottlenecks and rising prices.[4]

Running below capacity in any one year does not mean management should necessarily downsize its production plant. Production capacity is a long-run planning decision. Most manufacturers have some capacity in reserve to provide for growth. Even if the long-term forecast suggests that capacity should be reduced, it takes time to reduce fixed costs of capacity. The immediate question is how to determine product cost, given idle production capacity during the year.

Basically, there are two alternative methods when there is idle capacity: one ignores it, the one deals with it in the open. The Profit Profile and Manufacturing Cost Profile for each alternative are shown in Table 5-5.

The *actual output method* is virtually a carbon copy of the Profit Profile and Manufacturing Cost Profile presented earlier; the only change is that production capacity is 15,000 units. The actual production of 12,000 units is divided into the total fixed overhead costs of $2,100,000 to get the fixed overhead cost per unit, which is $175.00. This is called the *burden rate*. The logic of the actual-output method is that the actual number of units

---

[4]Martin Crutsinger, *(Boulder) Daily Camera*, 19 February 1988, p. 6B.

TABLE 5-5

MANUFACTCO's Profit Profile

Sales Volume For Year   11,000 units

	Actual Output Method		Capacity Based Method	
	Per Unit	Total	Per Unit	Total
Sales Revenue	$1,400.00	$15,400,000	$1,400.00	$15,400,000
Product Cost	$ (685.00)	$ (7,535,000)	$ (650.00)	$ (7,150,000)
Variable-Operating Expenses	$ (305.00)	$ (3,355,000)	$ (305.00)	$ (3,355,000)
Profit Margin	$ 410.00	$ 4,510,000	$ 445.00	$ 4,895,000
Fixed Operating Expenses		$ (2,300,000)		$ (2,300,000)
Idle Capacity Cost				$ (420,000)
Operating Profit		$ 2,210,000		$ 2,175,000

MANUFACTO's Manufacturing Cost Profile

Practical Production Capacity   15,000 units
Actual Output During Period   12,000 units

	Actual Output Method		Capacity Based Method	
	Total	Per Unit	Total	Per Unit
Raw Materials Costs	$2,580,000	$215.00	$2,580,000	$215.00
Direct Labor Costs	$3,120,000	$260.00	$3,120,000	$260.00
Variable Overhead Costs	$ 420,000	$ 35.00	$ 420,000	$ 35.00
Fixed Overhead Costs	$2,100,000	$175.00	$1,680,000	$140.00
Idle Capacity Cost			$ 420,000	
Total Manufacturing Costs	$8,220,000	$685.00	$8,220,000	$650.00

produced should absorb all fixed overhead costs for the year. Idle capacity is not charged with any of the fixed overhead costs.

In contrast, the capacity-based method divides the total fixed manufacturing overhead costs between the units produced and the units not produced (the idle capacity). The company had 20 percent idle capacity during the year, so 20 percent of the $2,100,000 total fixed overhead costs, or $420,000 is charged to the Idle Capacity Cost for year. Put another way, to determine product cost the fixed overhead burden rate is based on capacity, as follows:

**$2,100,000 fixed overhead/15,000 units capacity
= $140.00 burden rate**

This is $35 less than the burden rate of the actual output method. The product cost per unit thus drops from $685 to $650. Therefore, Cost-of-Goods-Sold Expense is lower by $35 per unit, or $385,000 lower for the 11,000 units sold during the year. On the other hand, $420,000 Idle Capacity Cost is charged to the year. The net difference is a $35,000 decrease in Operating Profit by the capacity-based method, compared with the actual-output method. So, one method versus the other does not make that much difference in operating profit, though the capacity-based method is a little more conservative.

The more important lesson is that managers should keep alert to which method is being used to determine product cost per unit, which in turn affects the profit margin per unit. Many managers favor the actual-output method because it keeps *all* the fixed manufacturing overhead cost in the product cost. They don't like treating idle-capacity cost as a separate expense. From the Manufacturing Cost Profile the manager can see clearly that the business produced at only 80 percent of its capacity, and that product cost per unit is higher based on actual output than it would be based on capacity.

If in fact the business had operated at full capacity and manufactured 15,000 units, the fixed overhead burden rate would have been $140 per unit, and product cost would have been $650 per unit. Reporting the capacity-based product cost per unit, for comparison with the actual-output-based figure, could be useful. The capacity-based product cost is the "ideal" or optimal cost that might be a better benchmark for setting sales price, and for comparing product cost trends year to year.

Suppose MANUFACTCO's actual output had been only 75 percent or 70 percent of production capacity. The results would not be that different from that shown in the Profit and Manufacturing Cost Profiles for the 80 percent output case. But, what about extreme cases where actual output is less than 50 percent of production capacity? The fixed overhead burden rate based on actual output would be too high; total fixed overhead costs would be spread over too few units of output. The product costs per unit would become too high. Idle capacity cost would have to be recorded. Product cost should be based on a normal output level, not necessarily equal to 100 percent of production capacity necessarily, but usually in the 75–90 percent range of capacity.

VARIABLE MANUFACTURING COST INEFFICIENCIES

The ideal manufacturing scenario is one of maximum production efficiency: no wasted materials, no wasted labor, no excessive reworking of products that don't pass inspection the first time through, no unnecessary power usage, and so on. The goal is optimum efficiency for all variable costs of production.

The management accounting reporting system should highlight productivity ratios for each manufacturing factor—each raw material item, each labor step, and each variable cost factor. One key productivity ratio, for instance, is the direct labor hours per product manufactured. For instance, a recent article in *The New York Times* reports:

> David M. Roderick, its chief executive, said USX now makes a ton of steel in less than 4 man-hours, down from 10 a few years ago.[5]

The computation of product cost per unit is based on the premise that the manufacturing process is reasonably efficient, in other words, that the productivity ratios for every variable manufacturing cost factor are fairly close to what they should be.

However, what if there were gross inefficiencies during the period? Managers should become aware of these in the monthly (perhaps weekly) production-control reports, and should take quick action to deal with the problems. But there is the problem

---

[5]Claudia H. Deutsch, "U.S. Industry's Unfinished Struggle," *The New York Times*, 21 February 1988, Sec. 3, p. 1, col. 4.

of how to deal with the excess, non-productive costs in determining product cost.

To illustrate, suppose that MANUFACTCO wasted raw materials cost during the year; its $2,580,000 total cost of raw materials includes $660,000 wastage. This may have been caused by inexperienced or untrained employees, or it may be that inferior quality materials were not up to its product quality control standards. This problem should have been stopped before it amounted to so much; quicker action should have been taken. In any case, assume the problem persisted and the result was that raw materials costing $660,000 had to be thrown away and replaced during the year.

As with idle capacity, there are two basic methods to deal with variable manufacturing cost inefficiencies: one method ignores it and the other deals with it as a separate factor. The Profit Profile and Manufacturing Cost Profile for each method are shown in Table 5–6 (production capacity is set equal to actual output to isolate on the variable cost inefficiency).

Notice that product cost per unit is $55 lower by the standard-based method; the excess-raw-materials cost is separated out and not included in product cost. Thus, Cost of Goods Expense is $605,000 less (11,000 units sold times the $55). But, the $660,000 excess raw materials cost is deducted as expense in the year, so the net effect is to reduce operating profit $55,000. Not a very large difference in operating profit, to be certain. However, the $55 difference in product cost per unit—$685 by the actual cost method versus $630 by the standard based method—is the more significant difference to managers. Product cost is the basic reference point for making sales price and other decisions. Clearly, managers should know whether the actual-cost method or the standard-based method is being used to determine the variable cost components of product cost.

For planning and control, many manufacturing businesses use standard cost systems, which are discussed in Chapter 11. Under these systems standards for raw materials, direct labor, and variable overhead costs are established, and variances (deviations) from the set standards are recorded. The standard-based method, shown in the Profit and Manufacturing Cost Profiles above, is relatively easy to implement when the manufacturer has a standard-cost system.

TABLE 5-6

MANUFACTCO's Profit Profile

Sales Volume For Year   11,000 units

	Actual Cost Method		Standard Based Method	
	Per Unit	Total	Per Unit	Total
Sales Revenue	$1,400.00	$15,400,000	$1,400.00	$15,400,000
Product Cost	$ (685.00)	$ (7,535,000)	$ (630.00)	$ (6,930,000)
Variable-Operating Expenses	$ (305.00)	$ (3,355,000)	$ (305.00)	$ (3,355,000)
Profit Margin	$ 410.00	$ 4,510,000	$ 465.00	$ 5,115,000
Fixed Operating Expenses		$ (2,300,000)		$ (2,300,000)
Excess Raw Materials Cost				$ (660,000)
Operating Profit		$ 2,210,000		$ 2,155,000

MANUFACTO's Manufacturing Cost Profile

Practical Production Capacity   12,000 units
Actual Output During Period   12,000 units

	Actual Cost Method		Standard Based Method	
	Total	Per Unit	Total	Per Unit
Raw Materials Costs	$2,580,000	$215.00	$1,920,000	$160.00
Excess Raw Materials Cost			$ 660,000	
Direct Labor Costs	$3,120,000	$260.00	$3,120,000	$260.00
Variable Overhead Costs	$ 420,000	$ 35.00	$ 420,000	$ 35.00
Fixed Overhead Costs	$2,100,000	$175.00	$2,100,000	$175.00
Total Manufacturing Costs	$8,220,000	$685.00	$8,220,000	$630.00

However, many manufacturers do not use any formal standard cost system. Nevertheless, managers should test actual costs against some benchmark of performance, even if there are no formal standards as such. In short, gross inefficiencies of materials, labor, and variable overhead should not be included in product cost.

EXCESSIVE PRODUCTION

Please refer again to MANUFACTCO's Profit Profile and Manufacturing Cost Profile: See Table 5–3. Notice the $2,100,000 total fixed manufacturing overhead cost for the year. Only $1,925,000 is included in Cost-of-Goods-Sold Expense for the year. The fixed overhead burden rate is $175 per unit. Only 11,000 of the 12,000 units produced during the year were sold, so only [11,000 units × $175 burden rate = $1,925,000] is allocated to Cost-of-Goods-Sold Expense. The other $175,000 of fixed overhead cost [$2,100,000 less the $1,925,000 in Cost-of-Goods-Sold Expense] is allocated to the inventory increase [$175 burden rate × 1,000 units inventory increase = $175,000].

Generally accepted accounting principles require that a proportionate share of the year's total fixed manufacturing overhead cost be allocated to the inventory increase during the year. Remember that inventory cost is not recorded as expense until the goods are sold in the future. The inclusion of fixed overhead costs in inventory is called the *full-cost absorption method*. In short, very often production capacity must be enough for the sales made during the year *and* to increase inventory for the sales growth forecast for next year.

However, sometimes a manufacturer makes too many products; production output is much more than sales volume for the period. Thus, there is a large increase in inventory, much more than would be needed for next year. Suppose, for example, that MANUFACTO sold only 6,000 units during the year, even though it manufactured 12,000 units. Its inventory would have increased 6,000 units, as many units as it sold during the year. This could be in anticipation of a long strike looming in the near future, which could shut down production for several months. Or, perhaps the company predicts serious shortages of raw material parts during the next several months. There could be such legitimate reasons for a large inventory build up. But, assume not.

Instead, assume the company fell far short of its sales goals for the year and failed to adjust its production output. The large inventory "overhang" at year-end presents all sorts of problems. Where to store it? Will sales price have to be cut to move the inventory? What about the fixed manufacturing overhead cost included in inventory? This last question is one managers might not think about.

If only 6,000 units had been produced, the company would have had 50 percent idle capacity, a problem discussed earlier in the chapter. By producing 12,000 units, the company seems to be making full use of its production capacity. But is it really? Producing excessive inventory is a false or illusory use of production capacity.

A good case can be made that fixed manufacturing overhead costs should not be included in any *excess* inventory. The basic argument is that the amount of fixed overhead cost allocated to the excess inventory should be treated the same as idle-capacity cost, and be charged off as expense. Unless the company were to slash its fixed overhead costs, which is very difficult to do in the short-run, it will have these fixed costs again next year. Next year, when the company downsizes its inventory, it will have idle-capacity cost. So, why not recognize the idle capacity cost this year instead of waiting until next year?

As a practical matter it is very difficult to draw the line between excessive inventory and normal (desirable) inventory levels. Unless ending inventory were very large, the full-cost absorption method would be used, which means the fixed overhead burden rate would be included in the product cost of the excess inventory. In any case, the manager should be aware that the product cost includes this fixed overhead burden rate. The more urgent problem facing the manager is to correct the inventory level, to bring it into more normal balance with projected sales volumes.

A FINAL NOTE: MULTIPLE PRODUCTS AND OVERHEAD-BURDEN RATES

Instead of just one product, assume MANUFACTCO makes twenty or more different products in its one production plant.

For each product the business must keep detailed records which accumulate the raw materials and direct labor used from the beginning to the end of the manufacturing process for each product. This requires an enormous amount of meticulously detailed bookkeeping that matches up the direct costs with each batch of products. Manufacturing overhead costs are quite another matter.

By their very nature overhead costs are *non-direct* costs. They cannot be matched up, or directly connected with any particular batch of products, or work station, or production department. Consider the annual salary of the production vice president or the annual property tax on the production plant property for instance. Neither can be coupled with any one batch of products, nor the work stations or departments the products move through in the manufacturing process. Overhead costs, therefore, have to be allocated or apportioned in some manner.

The business must identify a *common denominator* among its products that would be a good basis for allocating its manufacturing-overhead costs. Often direct-labor hours is the most practical common denominator because all products require direct labor. However, at a recent meeting in Chicago a partner with Arthur Andersen, the international accounting and consulting firm, said that based on studies and his own experience that direct labor is often 15 percent or less of total manufacturing cost. He mentioned that raw materials often is 50 percent or more of total product cost. So, perhaps some measure of materials would be a better common denominator of overhead cost allocation.

Whatever the basis of allocation, the manager should be aware that the allocation is bound to be somewhat of an arbitrary choice, which means that some products might be favored and others penalized. In short, the manager should take both the variable and fixed-overhead-cost components of product cost with a grain of salt. One product could be made to look unprofitable (or more profitable) merely by changing the basis of allocating overhead cost.

CHAPTER 6

PROFIT PATROL

A successful formula for making profit can take a wrong turn anytime. Every step on the pathway to profit is slippery. Managers have to keep constant watch. The theme of this chapter is in its title: Managers should patrol profit. Managers should keep a keen lookout on all profit factors, as well spot opportunities for profit improvement. Nothing can be taken for granted. A popular term these days is "environmental scan," which is a good term here also. Managers should make profit radar scans to see if there are any blips on the screen that signal trouble.

The chapter starts with the profile of a *loser,* a business suffering an operating loss instead of making profit. The lessons of previous chapters are applied to analyze the reason(s) for the loss, and to identify which factor(s) must be improved to turn the situation around. Basically the question is, "What's wrong?" Managers obviously must know the answer to this question.

Often the answer is found in the "frustrating fringe" surrounding the basic pathway to profit. This broad term refers to several different negative pressures on profit that managers have to deal with day in and day out. These are sinkholes and pitfalls on the pathway to profit. For instance, sales prices are subject to discounts. Product cost is subject to the additional expense of inventory shrinkage. These are just two examples of the many negative pressures on operating profit.

Many businesses sell two or more different products or product lines. Generally, the profit margins on each product or product line are considerably different. Thus, the analysis of *sales mix* and shifts in sales mix are important. Also, multiple products and product lines usually share a common base of fixed expenses. Different sales revenue sources benefit from one central pool of fixed opearating expenses.

A key management question is whether or not to allocate the fixed expenses among the products or product lines. Allocation may appear to be a good idea. But, *how* does allocation help decision making? This is a controversial question, especially where each product line is a separate profit center of the business for which the product manager has profit responsibility and whose compensation may depend (in part at least) on profit performance.

THE PROFILE OF A LOSER—OR, HOW TO TURN LOSS INTO PROFIT

Profile of Operating Loss

Suppose you're the manager in charge of a division, or territory, or product line of a business. (For that matter you may be the owner/manager of a small business.) Table 6–1 shows the Profit Profile for the most recent year.

As the manager with profit responsibility you have already taken a lot of heat from corporate headquarters for the $145,000 operating loss. Your job is to turn things around, and fairly fast. Your next year-end bonus, and perhaps keeping your job, depends on it.

TABLE 6–1
Profit Profile For LOSSCO

Annual Sales Volume	100,000 units	
Annual Break-even Volume	120,000 units	
Annual Capacity Volume	150,000 units	
	Per Unit	Total
Sales Revenue	$ 50.00	$ 5,000,000
Product Cost	$(32.50)	$(3,250,000)
Variable Expenses	$(10.25)	$(1,025,000)
Profit Margin	$ 7.25	$ 725,000
Fixed Expenses		$ (870,000)
Operating Profit (Loss)		$ (145,000)

First: Some Questions About Fixed Expenses

One thing you might do first is to question or at least to take a closer look at the $870,000 total fixed expenses included in your Profit Profile. This doesn't directly address the problem of how to turn things around and make an operating profit. But a couple of points require brief discussion before proceeding.

It's possible that you have argued in the past for a reduction of fixed expenses on the grounds that capacity is too high relative to your sales volume forecasts. Your capacity is 150,000 units compared with a sales of only 100,000 units; sales volume uses only ⅔ of capacity. Perhaps you were overridden on this point and are still being charged with fixed expenses for capacity that you really don't want. The cost of excess capacity is an obvious place to cut costs, which is examined later.

Your fixed expenses of $870,000 may be in total or in part an *allocated* amount from a larger pool of fixed expenses of corporate headquarters or from a larger organizational unit of the business that your sub-unit reports to. The basis of allocation is always open to question; allocation is always somewhat arbitrary. For instance, consider the legal expenses of the business. How should these be allocated to each profit center throughout the organizational structure of the business? Likewise, what about the centralized data processing and accounting expenses of the business? Many fixed expenses are allocated on some arbitrary basis that is open to question.

However, questions about the proper basis of allocation should be settled *before* the end of the year. Raising such questions after the fact, i.e., after the profit and loss results are in for the period, is too late. In any case, if you argue for less (a smaller allocation of fixed expenses to your unit), then you are also arguing that some other unit should get more of the fixed expenses, which will initiate a counter argument from that unit. Also, it may appear that you're making excuses rather than fixing the problem(s).

There is another very important management question about fixed expenses. Whether you're the owner/manager of a business or a profit center manager in a larger business, you should take a hard look at the specific items making up the total fixed expenses. In particular, is there is a significant amount of *depreciation expense* included in the total?

Depreciation is not a cash outlay expense during the period. As you know, depreciation expense is based on cost of assets; a certain fraction of original cost is allocated to each year. Accountants treat depreciation as a fixed expense based on formulas that allocate original cost over the estimated useful economic lives of the assets. For instance, under current income tax laws, buildings are depreciated over 31.5 years, and cars and light trucks over 5 years. Just because accountants adopt such methods doesn't mean that depreciation is **in fact** a fixed expense.

Contrast depreciation, for example, with annual property taxes on buildings and land. Property tax is a cash outlay each year. The tax is the cost to the business of police and fire protection and other governmental services by the city or county. Whether or not the business made full use of the building and land during the year, the entire amount of tax should be charged to the year as fixed expense. There's no argument about this. But depreciation raises entirely different issues.

Suppose the operating loss is due primarily to a lower volume of operations. You can argue that less depreciation should be charged to expense in the year, and that difference should be shifted to future years. The reasoning is that the assets were not used as much—the machines were not operated as many hours, the trucks not driven as many miles, and so on. In contrast, some assets depreciate mainly with the passage of time. For instance, depreciation of computers used in the accounting department is based on an expected technological life of the computers. Using the computers less doesn't delay the date of replacing the computers.

Generally speaking, arguing for less depreciation is not going to get you very far. Most businesses are not willing to make such a radical change in their depreciation policies, i.e., to slow down depreciation charges if sales volume slows down. Also, this would look suspicious as if the business were manipulating its recorded profit. In any case, the manager should be aware of the method of calculating depreciation expense that is included in total fixed expenses for the period. And, the manager should keep in mind that depreciation is not a cash outlay during the period. (The cash flow dynamics of profit [and loss] are examined in Chapter 8.)

What's The Problem?

Let's look at the $145,000 operating loss by following the basic pathway illustrated earlier in the book. See Table 6–2.

Which of the three basic determinants of operating profit (or loss) is the main problem here: the profit margin per unit, sales volume, or total fixed expenses? If profit margin per unit is the problem, which of its determinants is the problem: sales price, product cost, or variable expenses?

The analysis techniques explained in previous chapters point the way and suggest possible answers; analysis techniques are the best place to start solving the causes of the operating loss. If you had to hazard a guess here, what would you say is the main problem, or the principal cause of the operating loss? Assume, for instance, you are asked by the manager, a friend of yours, to look at the "numbers," and, without knowing much more, to give a quick appraisal of the operating loss. At what would you point your finger? Not so easy, is it? Some basic analysis is needed.

You could change each factor 10 percent for the better to see which would make the most improvement and whether any of these 10 percent changes would take the business from loss to profit. You could do trade-off analysis to see if any of these tactics would pull the business out of the red into the black. You could determine how many more units would have to be sold to

TABLE 6–2
Computation of Operating Loss

Sales Price	$ 50.00		
Product Cost	$(32.50)		
Variable Expenses	$(10.25)		
Profit Margin	$ 7.25		
	×		
	100,000 units	=	Total Profit Margin $725,000
	Sales Volume		Total Fixed Expenses $(870,000)
			Operating Profit (Loss)
			$(145,000)

get the business up to its break-even point. Let's start with this computation:

<u>Additional Sales Volume Needed Just To Break-even</u>
$145,000 Operating Loss/$7.25 Profit Margin Per Unit
= 20,000 Units

The business would have had to sell 20,000 additional units just to break-even. Sales volume would have to increase 20 percent. In fact, the Profit Profile (See Table 6–1) reports the break-even volume, which is 120,000 units.

What's even more important is that break-even is **80** percent of capacity:

<u>Break-even As Percent Of Capacity</u>
120,000 Units Breakeven/150,000 Units Capacity = 80%

I would say that this points to the main problem. Break-even should not be such a high percent of capacity. This means that the profit margin per unit should be higher. Recall that break-even is computed as follows:

<u>Computation of Break-even</u>
Total Fixed Expenses/Profit Margin Per Unit = Break-even
$870,000/$7.25 = 120,000 units

Suppose the profit margin slips a little more; say it drops $1.45 to only $5.80 per unit. At this level the business would have to sell its capacity to break-even:

<u>Total Fixed Expenses/Profit Margin Per Unit = Break-even</u>
$870,000/$5.80 = 150,000 units

In short, the manager needs to improve the profit margin per unit.

Assume the business wants to earn an operating profit equal to 15.0 percent of its sales revenue, which many successful businesses achieve (for example, Coca Cola as mentioned at the start of Chapter 1). Well, the business can't do it. Profit margin per unit is only 14.5 percent of sales price [$7.25 Profit Margin/ $50.00 sales price = 14.5%]. And, this is *before* fixed expenses are considered. To show the impact of this point, suppose the business had sold at full capacity or 150,000 units. (See Table 6–3).

Even at full capacity, operating profit is just $217,500, which is only 2.9 percent of sales revenue. By almost any standard or benchmark of comparison, 2.9 percent profit is seriously inadequate. For one thing, profit-making operations require a substantial amount of assets, as the next chapter explains. The capital invested in assets is supplied by debt and equity sources, i.e., lenders and stockholders. Debt alone may cost a business 3.0 percent of its sales revenue, to say nothing about the cost of equity.

So, the manager's top priority should be to improve the profit margin per unit. Increasing sales volume 20 percent, which is a large increase, would only take the business up to the break-even point. A 50 percent increase—a huge increase—would result in only a 2.9 percent return on sales (before interest and income tax). The other basic alternative would be to reduce fixed operating expenses.

Assume, for instance, that the business could slash its fixed expenses by one third ($290,000) and this would reduce its capacity by one third or down to 100,000 units. The result is shown in Table 6–4. Operating profit would be $145,000, which is much better than a loss. But this is still only a 2.9 percent return on

TABLE 6–3
Sales Volume Equals Capacity

Profit Profile For LOSSCO

Annual Sales Volume	150,000 units	
Annual Break-even Volume	120,000 units	
Annual Capacity Volume	150,000 units	
	Per Unit	*Total*
Sales Revenue	$ 50.00	$ 7,500,000
Product Cost	$(32.50)	$(4,875,000)
Variable Expenses	$(10.25)	$(1,537,500)
Profit Margin	$ 7.25	$ 1,087,500
Fixed Expenses		$ (870,000)
Operating Profit (Loss)		$ 217,500

TABLE 6–4
Fixed Expenses Reduced By One Third

Profit Profile For LOSSCO

Annual Sales Volume	100,000 units
Annual Break-even Volume	120,000 units
Annual Capacity Volume	100,000 units

	Per Unit	Total
Sales Revenue	$ 50.00	$ 5,000,000
Product Cost	$(32.50)	$(3,250,000)
Variable Expenses	$(10.25)	$(1,025,000)
Profit Margin	$ 7.25	$ 725,000
Fixed Expenses		$ (580,000)
Operating Profit (Loss)		$ 145,000

sales revenue, which is much too low as discussed before. In summary, it's fairly clear that the profit margin is too low.

Improving Profit Margin

Now for the tough question: How would you improve profit margin per unit? Is sales price too low? Or, are product cost and variable expenses too high? Do all three need improving? Answering these questions strikes at the heart of the manager's function. Managers are paid for knowing what to do and what has to be changed, as well as how to make the changes.

Analysis techniques don't provide the final answers to these questions, but these methods certainly help the manager to "size up" and quantify the impact of improvements in the profit-margin factors. One way to start is to analyze the impact of very modest improvements in each factor. Suppose, for instance, you could improve each factor by just one percent. Doesn't sound like much does it? But the combined effect would be to increase profit margin $.9275 per unit (see Table 6–5).

On 100,000 units sales volume this would yield $92,750 improvement. In short, each one percent of combined improvements has a total of $92,750 favorable impact. Say you could improve each factor 5 percent, there would be total improvement

TABLE 6-5

	One Percent Improvements		
	Old	New	Change
Sales Price	$50.00	$50.5000	$.5000
Product Cost	(32.50)	(32.1750)	.3250
Variable Expenses	(10.25)	(10.1475)	.1025
Profit Margin	$ 7.25	$ 8.1775	$.9275

of $463,750—from a loss of $145,000 to an operating profit of $318,750—as shown in Table 6-6.

However, even in this situation operating profit is only a little over 6 percent of sales revenue, far short of a 15 percent return on sales objective.

The manager could "load" all the needed improvements on one factor, such as the sales price. If all the improvements have to come from an increase in the sales price, you can determine what the new sales price would have to be to achieve a 15 percent return on sales revenue, assuming sales volume remains at 100,000 units. You have $42.75 expense per unit (product cost plus variable expense). And, you have $870,000 total fixed expenses, which is $8.70 per unit spread over the 100,000 units

TABLE 6-6
Five Percent Improvements in Each Profit Margin Factor

Profit Profile For LOSSCO

Annual Sales Volume	100,000 units
Annual Break-even Volume	73,186 units
Annual Capacity Volume	150,000 units

	Per Unit	Total
Sales Revenue	$ 52.50	$ 5,250,000
Product Cost	$(30.88)	$(3,087,500)
Variable Expenses	$ (9.74)	$ (973,750)
Profit Margin	$ 11.89	$ 1,188,750
Fixed Expenses		$ (870,000)
Operating Profit (Loss)		$ 318,750

sales volume. Total expense per unit is thus $51.45. This amount has to be 85 percent of sales price since you want to earn 15 percent return (Operating Profit) on sales.

Hence, sales price would have to be $60.53:

$$\$51.45 \text{ Total Expense Per Unit}/85\%$$
$$= \$60.53\text{: Sales Price (rounded)}$$

This is more than a 20 percent increase from the present $50.00 sales price. Such a large increase probably is not realistic, to say the least, and in fact may drive down sales volume.

In summary, to reach an operating profit goal such as 15 percent return on sales, a very large improvement (more than 20 percent) is needed in one factor. Alternatively, sizable improvements (more than 5 percent) would be needed in all three profit margin factors. It's possible that the sales price (or product cost) is out of control by more than 20 percent. However, there are probably several "negatives" at work, which leads to the next section.

THE FRUSTRATING FRINGE

The basic pathway to profit is surrounded by a "frustrating fringe" of negative factors that reduce the profit margin per unit, decrease sales volume, or increase fixed expenses, as shown in Exhibit 6–1.

As you can see, every basic factor in the inner core of the profit pathway is subject to one or more negative pressures. Even more fringe factors could be included; those shown are the most common ones.

Sales-Price Negatives

When eating in a restaurant you don't argue about the menu prices, or at the gas pump, or at the supermarket. On the other hand, sales-price negotiation is the way of life in many situations. Many businesses advertise or publish *list prices*. Examples are sticker prices on new cars, manufacturer's suggested retail

EXHIBIT 6-1
"Frustrating Fringe" of Negative Factors Surrounding Basic Pathway To Profit

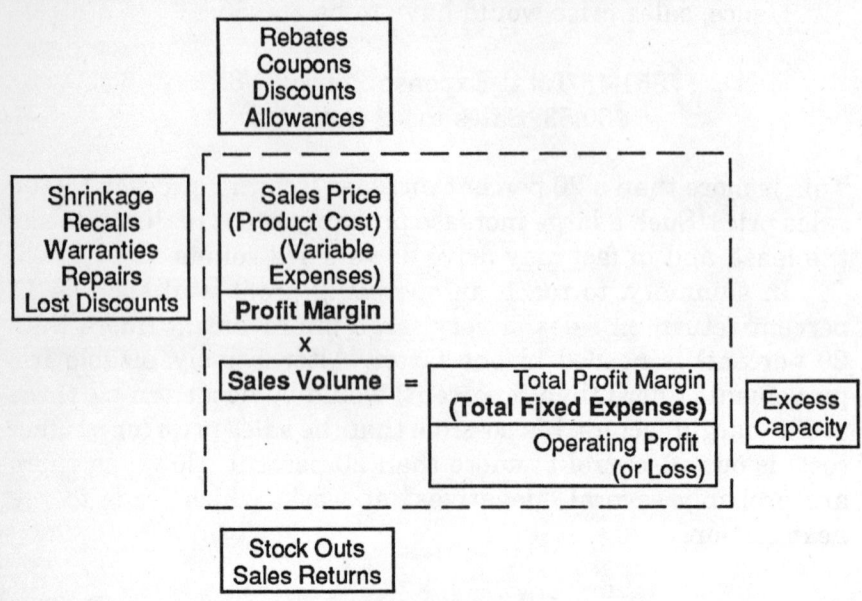

prices on many consumer products, and a standard price sheet for an entire industrial product line.

List prices are just the point of departure. In some cases, such as new car sales, neither the seller nor the buyer takes the list price as the real price; the list price simply sets the stage for bargaining. In many other cases, the buyer expects to pay list price, but subject to other types of price reductions.

Prompt payment discounts usually are offered when making sales on credit to other businesses, such as 2 percent for payment received within ten days. These are often called *sales discounts*, though as a buyer you should view them as penalties for delayed payment. Also, there are *quantity discounts* for large orders, and *special customer discounts*, such as for governmental and educational institutions.

Rebates and *coupons* are offered by many sellers, which lower the sales price. Sales price also may be reduced by giving *allowances* (or *adjustments*) after the point of sale if customers complain about the quality of the product or when minor product flaws are discovered by customers after taking delivery.

Managers should decide how these sales-price negatives will be recorded and reported to them. One extreme, not recommended, would be to record sales net of all such reductions. Only net sales prices and net total sales revenue for the period would be reported. The other extreme would be to record sales at list prices and accumulate sales revenue at gross (list) prices. Reductions would be recorded and accumulated in one or more *contra* accounts, which are deducted from gross sales revenue as shown in Table 6–7.

A business may not have all six of the contra accounts shown, although two, three, or four would not be unusual.

Without specific instructions from managers, the typical accounting system records some reductions in contra accounts, but not others. It's a mixed bag. Sales-price allowances and sales discounts are usually recorded in contra accounts, which means sales revenue is recorded at the sales prices *before* these two deductions. Rebates and coupons may also be recorded in contra accounts, though not necessarily. In contrast, quantity discounts and special customer discounts are generally not recorded; sales revenue is recorded at the "net" sales price (list price less the discount).

In external Income Statements, only net sales revenue is reported as a general rule of thumb. For internal reporting, however, gross sales revenue before all reductions should be recorded. Sales-price reductions should be accumulated in contra accounts, so managers can monitor each negative factor relative to established sales policies, for comparison with previous pe-

TABLE 6–7

Gross Sales Revenue (at list prices)		$10,000,000
Less: Sales Discounts	$150,000	
Special Customer Discounts	200,000	
Quantity (Volume) Discounts	375,000	
Rebates	725,000	
Coupons	165,000	
Price Allowances	82,000	(1,697,000)
Net Sales Revenue		$ 8,303,000

riods, and for comparison of actual performance against goals for the period.

Product Cost & Variable-Expense Negatives

Several factors increase product cost per unit and variable expense per unit sold, or per dollar of sales revenue. (See again Exhibit 6–1 which illustrates the frustrating fringe, in particular, the negative factors next to product cost and variable expenses.)

Inventory shrinkage is a serious problem for many businesses, especially retailers. Shrinkage is a polite term for shoplifting and employee theft, although the term sometimes includes other loss of inventory due to damage and deterioration. An analyst with Salomon Brothers, Inc. in a recent article in *The Wall Street Journal* states that "retailers' inventories shortages typically are 1.5% to 2% of sales."[1] Inventory shrinkage due to theft is a particularly frustrating expense. The business has to buy (or manufacture) the product, hold it in inventory (which requires carrying costs), only to have it stolen by a "customer" or an employee.

Internal controls and preventive measures help to minimize inventory shrinkage, but at a cost. Even elaborate and expensive controls cannot eliminate *all* inventory shrinkage. Almost every business has to tolerate some amount of shrinkage; preventing all shrinkage would be too costly or would offend customers and depress sales volume. Would you shop in a store that carried out body searches on all customers leaving the store? Many retailers hesitate about even requiring customers to check bags before entering their stores. AT&T got into trouble when it placed hidden microphones in its employees' restrooms to listen in on their conversations. On the other hand, closed circuit TV monitors are common in many stores. Inventory shrinkage is a never-ending problem.

Needless to say, product recalls can be costly. Abnormal warranty and repair costs add significant amounts to product cost or variable expenses of making sales. Lost discounts refer

---

[1] *The Wall Street Journal,* September 10, 1987, p. 4.

to those purchases made when the business fails to take advantage of prompt payment discounts, or buys in small quantities and forgoes volume (large quantity) discounts. Several other product cost and variable-expense negatives could be discussed. Only one is mentioned in passing here—higher than necessary purchase costs due to poor purchasing policies or due to purchasing agents accepting bribes, kickbacks, or other "favors" from vendors.

In internal profit reports to managers these negative factors should be accumulated in separate accounts for special attention. These costs should not be buried in cost-of-goods-sold expense or in variable-expense accounts. The manager may specifically have to instruct the accountant to isolate these costs. In external Income Statements these costs usually are included in a larger expense account, such as cost of goods sold, or general and administrative expense.

Sales-Volume Negatives

Sales returns can be a problem, although this varies considerably from industry to industry. Many retailers accept sales returns as good marketing policy. Customers may be refunded their money, or they may exchange for different products. Some products (such as new cars) are seldom returned (even when recalled). Generally, sales returns are accumulated in a separate contra account that is deducted from (gross) sales revenue, which is useful information for managers. In most external Income Statements to creditors and stockholders only net sales revenue (gross sales revenue less contra accounts is reported).

Lost sales due to temporary stock outs (zero inventory situations) are important for managers to know. However, such "non-sales" are not recorded; no sales transaction takes place, so there is nothing to record in the sales revenue account. Many times customers are willing to back order the products, or sales are made for future delivery. Of course, back orders and back logs should be recorded and reported to managers. However, if the customer refuses to back order, the sale may be lost forever. As a practical matter, it is difficult to keep track of lost sales; the manager may have to rely on other sources of information, such as complaints from customers and the sales force.

Excess Capacity

The problem of excess production capacity of manufacturers is discussed in Chapter 5, especially since it affects the determination of product cost. In addition, there may be excess *sales* capacity and excess *administrative/management* capacity. To put it another way, total fixed operating expenses often are too high relative to actual sales volume. The business has too much office space, too many employees, too many managers, too much retail space, too many delivery vehicles, and so on. Whereas production capacity is usually a "known" number, many businesses don't attempt to estimate either their sales capacity or administrative capacity.

Some ratios are helpful even if there is no measure of capacity as such. For example, many retailers keep an eye on *sales revenue per employee* and *sales revenue per square foot* of retail space. Most retailers have rough rules of thumb, such as $600 per square foot of retail space, or $150,000 per employee. These amounts differ from industry to industry. Trade associations collect such data from their members. Retailers can compare their performance against local and regional competition, as well as national averages. Hotels and motels carefully watch their *occupancy rates,* another example of a useful ratio for measuring excess sales capacity.

Reducing a fixed expense is not easy, to say the least. Employees have to be fired (or temporarily laid off), major assets have to be sold, and so on. Such "downsizing" are difficult decisions to make. For one thing they are an admission of the inability of the business to generate enough sales volume to justify the fixed expenses. Nonetheless, part of the manager's job is to make these painful decisions. The tendency is to put the decision off, to delay the tough choices that have to be made. Indeed, in a recent interview by *The Wall Street Journal* the retired CEO of Westinghouse, Douglas Danforth, in response to a question regarding the biggest failings of American chief executives said:

> "some of us tend to procrastinate. Even when our stomach tells us that we need to make a major change, some executives, in-

cluding myself, are reluctant to face up to those at the earliest possible time. That's just human nature."[2]

SALES MIX AND FIXED EXPENSES

Suppose you're the General Manager of a major division of SALESMIXCO, a diversified manufacturing business. Your division manufactures and sells one basic product line, consisting of four products sold under your label, plus one product sold as a generic (no label) product to a supermarket chain. Your *Product Line Profit Profile* for the most recent year is shown in Table 6–8. Both the dollar amounts and percents are presented. Fixed expenses are *not* allocated among the five products, although this alternative is discussed later.

All five products are earning a profit margin even though the unit profit margins vary both in dollar amount and percent across products. The Generic product has the highest percent of profit margin (46 percent), but the Premier product has the highest dollar amount of profit margin ($26.60). Production costs are cut to the bone on the Generic product and no advertising or sales promotion is done on the product; the variable expenses are mainly delivery costs. Product cost is the highest for the Premier product because the best raw materials are used and additional labor time is required to make its quality the top of the line. Also, advertising and sales promotion is heavy on this product; variable expenses are 24 percent of sales price.

Notice that the Economy model accounts for 18 percent of sales volume, but less than 10 percent of total profit margin. The Premier model accounts for only 9 percent of sales volume, but over 17 percent of total profit margin. Which brings up the very important issue of *sales mix*. Whenever two or more products are sold, the relative weights of each to overall profitability is a key variable for management analysis. In particular, shifts in sales mix and trade-offs among the products is important to understand.

---

[2]"Retiring Westinghouse Chief Executive Talks of Issues Facing Firms and Managers," *The Wall Street Journal*, December 30, 1987, p. 15.

TABLE 6-8
Product Line Profit Profile

	Generic	Economy	Standard (Product Line)	Deluxe	Premier	Averages/Totals
Sales Price	$ 28.25	$ 42.50	$ 60.00	$ 75.00	$ 95.00	$ 52.61
Product Cost	$ (14.13)	$ (28.05)	$ (36.00)	$ (39.00)	$ (45.60)	$ (29.61)
Variable Expense	$ (1.13)	$ (6.80)	$ (10.80)	$ (16.50)	$ (22.80)	$ (9.02)
Profit Margin/Unit	$ 13.00	$ 7.65	$ 13.20	$ 19.50	$ 26.60	$ 13.98
Sales Volume	28,000	18,000	35,000	10,000	9,000	100,000
Total Profit Margin	$363,860	$137,700	$462,000	$195,000	$239,400	$1,397,960
Fixed Expenses						$ (766,000)
Operating Profit						$ 631,960

	Generic	Economy	Standard (Product Line)	Deluxe	Premier	Averages/Totals
Sales Price	100.00%	100.00%	100.00%	100.00%	100.00%	100.00%
Product Cost	−50.00%	−66.00%	−60.00%	−52.00%	−48.00%	−56.28%
Variable Expense	−4.00%	−16.00%	−18.00%	−22.00%	−24.00%	−17.15%
Profit Margin/Unit	46.00%	18.00%	22.00%	26.00%	28.00%	26.57%
Sales Volume	28.00%	18.00%	35.00%	10.00%	9.00%	100.00%
Total Profit Margin	26.03%	9.85%	33.05%	13.95%	17.12%	100.00%

Sales Mix Trade-Offs

A basic marketing strategy of many businesses is to encourage their customers to "trade up" or to buy the higher-priced items in their product line. Higher-priced products generally have higher profit-margin percents. The newest products may have the highest profit margins. A recent article on Kodak quotes its Chairman and CEO, Colby Chandler: "We are a high margin company, and it is new products that have the highest margins."[3]

Compare the Standard versus the Deluxe products. You make $6.30 more profit margin per unit on the Deluxe product. Clearly,

---

[3] *The New York Times,* Sunday March 6, 1988, Section 3, p. 7.

you should be willing to give up one unit of Standard in trade for one unit of Deluxe. You even make more profit margin on the Generic product than on the Economy product. Marketing strategies should be based on profit-margin information such as presented in the Product Line Profit Profile.

The position of the Economy model is interesting because its profit margin is by far the lowest. The Economy model may be in the nature of a "loss leader"—a product you don't make much margin on, but one necessary to get the attention of customers, or one which serves as the stepping stone to customers to trade up to higher-priced products at a later time. Of course, the opposite may happen; in tough times many of your customers may trade down and buy products that yield lower profit margins. If large numbers of customers were down-trading to the Standard or Economy products, perhaps you should quickly raise the prices on these two models to protect your total profit margin.

Should you be making and selling the Generic product? This product brings in over 26 percent of your total profit margin. *On the other hand,* these units may be taking sales away from the other four products, though this is difficult to know for certain. If these Generic products were not available in the supermarkets, would these same customers buy one of your other models? If they all bought the Economy model, you would be much worse off; you'd be giving up sales on which you make a profit margin of $13.00 for units that earn only $7.65. However, if the customers shifted up to the Standard or better models, you would be ahead, even though customers who buy Generic products wouldn't seem the type of customer to trade up.

Many different marketing questions can be raised; indeed, the job of the manager is to consider the whole range of marketing strategies: positioning each product, setting sales prices, advertising, and so on. The analysis for deciding on sales strategy starts with a Product Line Profit Profile that reports profit margin and sales mix.

Fixed Expenses: To Allocate Or Not To Allocate?

One last question concerns whether or not to allocate total fixed expenses among the products. As discussed in Chapter 5, *pro-*

duction fixed costs must be allocated among the different products that are manufactured during the period. Please keep in mind that the product costs shown in the Product Line Profit Profile include manufacturing fixed costs, as well as materials and labor costs. The $766,000 is the total of *non-manufacturing* operating fixed expenses.

These fixed operating expenses generally fall into two broad categories: (1) sales and marketing expenses; and (2) general and administrative expenses. Most fixed operating expenses are indirect, which means the expenses cannot be directly associated or matched with a particular product. In fact, the SALESMIXCO example assumes there are no direct fixed expenses for any of the products. This, however, may not be true in some situations.

For example, an advertising campaign may feature only one product; suppose you bought a page in the *The New York Times* for the Premier product. The fixed cost of this one-time insertion should be deducted directly from the total profit margin of the Premier product. But, the majority of the fixed expenses are indirect. Should indirect fixed expenses be allocated among products?

You *can* allocate, although the basis for allocation is open to much debate and difference of opinion. For instance, you could allocate on the basis of sales volume (each unit sold gets equal fixed expense), or on the basis of sales revenue (each dollar of sales revenue gets equal fixed expense), or according to a more complex formula. But is allocation worth the effort? Does it help decision making?

The basic management question is whether you are making optimal use of your sales capacity and administrative/management capacity provided by the fixed expenses. This is a question of how to achieve the best profit-margin sales mix, which requires good marketing decisions. Allocation of indirect fixed expenses doesn't add anything to the marketing analysis.

A business may adopt incentive compensation plans, such as year-end bonuses, based on the operating profit for each product—not profit margin, but the operating profit after fixed expenses are deducted. In this situation fixed expenses would have to be allocated to determine the operating profit for each product.

Last, it should be mentioned also that a business may allocate fixed expenses to *minimize* the apparent operating profit on a product. I was hired to be an expert witness for the plaintiff in a patent infringement lawsuit against a well-known corporation. The defendant had already lost in the first stage; it had been found guilty of patent infringement. The corporation had manufactured and sold a product for three years that the plaintiff owned the patent to without compensating the plaintiff. The second stage was to assess the amount of damages to be awarded to the plaintiff.

The plaintiff was suing for recovery of all the profit made by the defendant corporation on sales of the product. The defendant allocated every cost it could think of to the product, including part of the CEOs annual salary, to minimize the profit it alleged was earned from sales of the product. The jury threw out such heavy-handed allocation, and finally awarded over $16 million to the plaintiff.

PART 2

THE FINANCIAL SIDE OF PROFIT

CHAPTER 7

WHY YOU NEVER SEE INCOME STATEMENTS WITHOUT BALANCE SHEETS

When I was going into seventh grade my father took a big risk. He quit a good paying job, moved our large family to Iowa, and started an office machines business selling and repairing typewriters and adding machines. Ten years later, when I was graduating from college, he was still in business. However, the business was in a precarious financial situation.

Since I majored in accounting and had just started working for a major CPA firm, my Dad would have me "look over" the books. He was making money, but he was taking too much of it out of the business too soon. A short time later he lost the business that he had worked so hard and so long to build.

My Dad was a great salesman. When home from college I used to travel with him on sales calls, and I observed a master salesman in action. But closing sales is not the end of the manager's job. Like many small business managers, he carefully read his Income Statement line by line, but he barely glanced at his Balance Sheet. He operated on two false assumptions:

1. If bottom line profit was good, then the financial condition of the business would naturally fall into place (somehow); and,
2. Bottom line profit (net income) was the amount of money you could take out of the business each year.

First of all, financial condition consists of a very diverse mix of assets and liabilities that do *not* automatically fall into place.

The Balance Sheet has to be managed as attentively as the Income Statement. Second, the Income Statement says *little to nothing* about cash flow. The next chapter explains the Cash Flow Statement, and why cash flow may be bad even if profit is good. This chapter explains how profit-making operations both depend on and drive the Balance Sheet.

THE BALANCE SHEET AND THE INCOME STATEMENT

It may not be any surprise to mention this, but you never see an Income Statement without a Balance Sheet. Your first reaction might be that both financial statements are needed. Obviously, the Income Statement is essential because it is the summary of revenues and expenses and the resulting profit (or loss) for the period.

The Balance Sheet is the summary of the assets, liabilities, and owner's equity that makes up the financial condition of the business. It provides information for comparing assets against liabilities, as well as the amounts of the external (capital stock) and internal (retained earnings) sources of the owner's equity in the business. Clearly, Balance Sheet information is needed for judging the solvency (debt-paying ability) of the business, and to determine the rate of return on equity earned by the business. Also, the Balance Sheet discloses the liquidity position of the business, which refers to its cash and cash equivalents-such as short-term investments, which can be immediately converted into cash.

All this is true. However, in my experience many managers make a critical mistake: they don't connect the Income Statement and the Balance Sheet. They don't seem to understand the mutual dependence and interactions between these two financial statements. This two-way street is illustrated in Exhibit 7–1.

The main driving forces behind the Balance Sheet are the profit-making operations of the business. The line of business you're in determines which kinds of assets you need. Airlines need jets, retailers need inventories, gambling casinos need a lot of money on hand, and so on. In turn, the flow of sales revenue and expenses change the assets and liabilities of the business.

EXHIBIT 7-1
Mutual Dependence & Interaction Between Income Statement and Balance Sheet

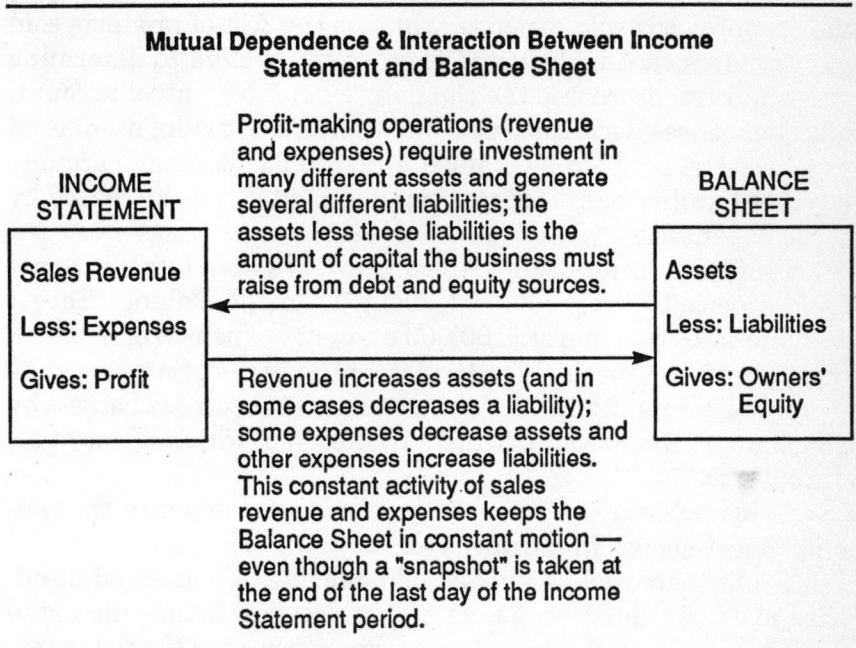

BASIC IMPACT OF PROFIT ON BALANCE SHEET

The Income Statement rests on the *profit equation*:

Sales Revenue − Expenses = Profit

In a parallel manner the Balance Sheet rests on the *financial condition equation* (also called the accounting equation):

Assets − Liabilities = Owners' Equity

Owners' Equity is separated into its two sources: (1) *paid-in capital,* which is the amount invested in the business by the owners; and (2) *retained earnings,* which is increased by profit and decreased by withdrawal of profit from the business, such as dividends paid to stockholders of corporations.

Sales revenue increases an asset, either cash, or accounts receivable when sales are made on credit.[1] Some expenses decrease assets; other expenses increase liabilities. For example, the cost-of-goods-sold expense, which is the cost of products sold to customers that is deducted from sales revenue to determine gross margin, decreases the company's inventory-asset account. Many expenses decrease cash. However, a surprising number of expenses are not paid for immediately; thus, either an accounts payable liability or an accrued expenses liability is increased by these expenses.

Profit means total sales revenue is more than total expenses for the period. But what does profit do to the Balance Sheet? Assume sales revenue of $100,000 and total expenses of $90,000; thus, profit (net income) is $10,000 for the period. Sales revenue increased assets $100,000. Assume expenses decreased assets by $80,000 and increased liabilities by $10,000, which is not at all unrealistic.

Sales revenue and expenses caused the changes in the Balance Sheet shown in Exhibit 7-2.

Profit increased assets $20,000, but it also increased liabilities $10,000. Thus, *net* assets (assets less liabilities) increased $10,000. Profit, in the most basic terms, increases the net assets of the business. Which assets? In particular, did *cash* increase $10,000? In other words, is profit money in the bank?

The Income Statement does not report *which* assets and liabilities are changed by sales revenue and expenses. In particular, there's no way to determine the cash flow from profit or even if it's positive or negative from the information in the Income Statement.

Cash flow from profit is reported in the *Cash Flow Statement*. This third and extremely important financial statement is explained in the next chapter. The remainder of this chapter explains the connections between sales revenue and expenses and

---

[1]Sometimes sales revenue is earned by delivery of a product or service previously paid for by customers; two examples are magazine publishers and airlines. Cash was received before the magazine was delivered or before the ticket was used. In these cases, sales revenue decreases a liability, the liability being the amount collected in advance from customers that would have to be refunded if the proudct or service were not delivered.

EXHIBIT 7-2
Changes in Balance Sheet Caused by Profit

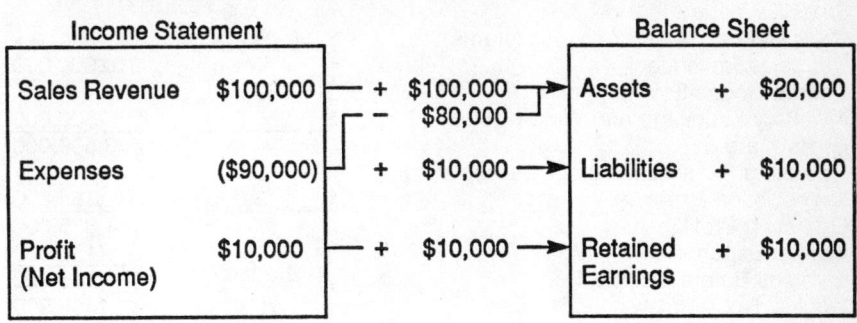

their *specific* assets and liabilities. This lays the foundation for the cash flow chapter which follows.

In short, managers must clearly understand the Balance Sheet effects of sales revenue and expenses. This is absolutely critical for understanding the Balance Sheet because most of the assets and liabilities in the Balance Sheet are the causes or effects of the profit-making operations of a business. Only a few liabilities are from borrowing money, and owner's equity boils down to only two basic accounts: paid-in capital and retained earnings. To manage financial condition and to plan finances and budgets, the Balance Sheet should be approached as the "supporting cast" for the main characters—sales revenue and expenses.

A PROFIT-MAKING VIEW OF THE BALANCE SHEET

The manager's primary financial objective is to make profit. Therefore, the manager should take a profit-making attitude towards the Balance Sheet. Fundamentally, this means knowing which assets are necessary to make profit and which liabilities result from making profit.

Income Statement Example

The Income Statement shown in Table 7-1 serves as our example to build up the Balance Sheet:

TABLE 7–1
Income Statement for Year

Sales Revenue	$10,500,000	
Sales Returns, Allowances, & Returns	$ (500,000)	
Net Sales Revenue		$10,000,000
Cost-of-Goods-Sold Expense	$ 6,250,000	
Inventory Shrinkage and Write-downs	$ 250,000	$ (6,500,000)
Gross Margin		$ 3,500,000
Operating Expenses, except Depreciation	$ 1,850,000	
Depreciation Expense	$ 315,000	$ (2,165,000)
Operating Profit		$ 1,335,000
Interest Expense		$ (150,000)
Earnings Before Income Tax		$ 1,185,000
Income Tax		$ (402,900)
Net Income		$ 782,100

This example is for a retailer or manufacturer. In other words, the business sells products. Notice the cost-of-goods-sold expense. The company experiences inventory shrinkage and writes down its obsolete products that have little or no sales value. Next, notice the deductions from sales revenue. After the point of sale the business gives price discounts and allowances and also accepts some returns from its customers; these are deducted from sales revenue to arrive at net-sales revenue.

These "negative factors" are discussed in Chapter 6. However, it should be mentioned here that in *external* Income Statements, in contrast to the internal profit reports to managers, sales discounts, returns, and allowances usually are not reported; only net sales revenue is disclosed. Likewise, inventory shrinkage and write-downs are not reported separately, but are "buried" in the larger cost-of-goods-sold expense amount. Most companies are very sensitive about divulging these negative factors in their external Income Statements. And they are not required to by generally accepted accounting principles.

Once you get below the gross margin line (also called gross profit), the patterns and details of disclosure in external Income Statements vary quite a bit. Only one general "catch-all" Operating Expenses account is shown in the example above. Instead, many companies report two or three classes of expenses, such as Marketing, General & Administrative, etc. However, these two or three also are very broad categories. Internal management profit reports contain literally hundreds of lines for operating expenses.

Notice in the Income Statement that depreciation expense is reported separate from the operating expenses. Interest and income tax expenses are always reported on separate lines, as shown in Table 7–1.

Sales Revenue And Expenses ↔ Cash

As you know, cash is the lubricant of business transactions; sooner or later virtually every revenue and expense passes through the cash account. It's the "sooner or later" that managers have to pay attention to. The Cash Flow Statement is absolutely critical to managers, and is examined in the next chapter. At this point, our concern is more limited: What amount of operating cash is needed to support the sales revenue and expense activity of this business?

Just how much cash would you keep in the till (the company's checking account) to pay bills as they come due, to meet your payroll, to provide for unexpected demands, and so on? There's no simple or standard answer. There's a very wide variety of opinion and practice on cash balances.

Some corporations such as IBM and Ford carry extremely large Cash balances; their Cash balances may be 20 percent or more of annual sales. (Cash includes temporary short-term investments in very liquid securities that can be converted into cash on a moment's notice.) Few companies are in a position to carry such a large cash balance. Some are on the edge of insolvency and need to open their mail each day to see what bills *can* be paid.

We'll assume a modest cash balance, say $400,000, which is only 4 percent of the $10,000,000 annual sales. So

Sales Revenue & Expenses ↔ $400,000 Cash

Sales Revenue ↔ Accounts Receivable

Assume the business sells on credit; cash is not received at the point of sale, but is collected later according to the credit terms offered to its customers. Credit sales increase the asset called

Accounts Receivable. The balance in this account is the amount of uncollected sales revenue.

By the end of the year most of the credit sales should have been collected. But the last few weeks of sales revenue would still be in Accounts Receivable at year-end. How many weeks (or days)? This obviously depends on the customer credit policies and collection experience of the company. For our example let's assume that $1,000,000 is uncollected at year-end, so

$10,000,000 Net Sales ↔ $1,000,000 Accounts Receivable

For control purposes, managers should closely monitor past-due accounts, i.e., those beyond the credit terms offered customers. Also, an estimate should be made for uncollectible (doubtful) customers' amounts included in the total of Accounts Receivable. Almost all companies that sell on credit experience some bad debts. The $1,000,000 is net of the reduction for uncollectible receivables.

Cost-of-Goods-Sold Expense ↔ Inventory and Accounts Payable

Almost all companies that sell products have to carry an inventory or stock of products ready for sale and delivery to their customers. The inventory holding period may be short (a few weeks or less) or fairly long (a few months or more). Supermarkets and gas stations are examples of high turnover (short holding periods). Retail furniture stores, art galleries, and most manufacturers are examples of low turnover (long holding periods).

The longer the holding period, the higher the profit margin as a general rule of thumb. In our example, the profit margin is 35 percent of net sales ($3,500,000 gross margin ÷ $10,000,000 net sales = 35%). This mid-range profit margin implies a mid-range holding period, say perhaps two or three months. We'll assume inventory is $1,375,000; this is about eleven weeks of annual sales.[2] So

---

[2]Cost-of-goods-sold expense for the year is $6,250,000. Remember that this is the *cost* of the goods sold, whose sales value is in the sales revenue account. Inventory is carried at cost, not sales value. Therefore, $6,250,000 ÷ 52 weeks = $120,192 per week, which times 11 weeks equals $1,322,115, and this is rounded off to $1,325,000 in the example.

$6,500,000 Cost-of-Goods-Sold Expense ↔
$1,375,000 Inventory

Most companies purchase inventory on credit, although the credit terms usually are shorter than the inventory holding period. Thus, the amount owed for inventory credit purchases is much less than inventory. The amount owed for credit purchases of inventory is recorded in the *Accounts Payable* liability account. This is a non-interest bearing liability, although if the liability goes past due there may be an interest penalty charged. Assume that the liability for inventory purchases on credit is $450,000 in this example; so

$1,375,000 Inventory ↔ $450,000 Accounts Payable

Operating Expenses ↔ Prepaid Expenses, Accounts Payable, and Accrued Expenses

Operating expenses, as you see in the sub-heading, are a little more involved than you may have thought. Many operating expenses are paid in cash, more or less on the pay-as-you-go basis. But, many have to be prepaid, such as insurance, office supplies, travel advances, and so on. Almost every business has these *Prepaid Expenses,* which are held in this asset account until the costs are used up and charged to Operating Expenses over time.

Instead of being prepaid, many operating expenses are bought on credit, such as telephone, utilities, legal and CPA fees, etc. *Accounts Payable* is increased by these expenses. (Recall that inventory credit purchases are also recorded in Accounts Payable.)

Many operating expenses are based on the gradual accumulation of costs that are to be paid only once or twice a year. A prime example is the accumulation of vacation time by employees. Week by week the employees accumulate credit towards their vacation to be taken later. Real estate property taxes which are paid in arrears, i.e., after the end of the tax year, is another example of the gradual accumulation of an expense that should be recognized in a liability account.

Product warranty and guarantee costs are yet another example of costs that accrue, or accumulate during the period although not paid until later, perhaps several months later. The accountant does not wait until such costs are paid to record the expense. In order to record the expense in the same period that the benefit occurs, the accountant records the expense with an increase to the *Accrued Expenses* liability account.

To sum up, Operating Expenses are interconnected with one asset and two liabilities as follows:

$1,850,000 Operating Expenses ↔ $185,000 Prepaid Expenses
$290,000 Accounts Payable
$415,000 Accrued Expenses

Of course, the dollar amounts of each of these three Balance Sheet accounts would vary from business to business. The ratio of each account to total operating expenses tends to remain fairly constant over time. These are reasonable ratios for this example, but, as just said, would vary for each business. For instance, the $415,000 Accrued Expenses are about 22 percent of the $1,850,000 Operating Expenses, but this might be lower or higher depending on many factors.

Depreciation Expense ↔ Fixed Assets

All businesses need *fixed assets,* a broad category that includes land, buildings, vehicles, computers, tools, equipment, machinery, and so on. To be honest, the term "fixed" is not the preferred description for these long-lived assets, and in fact you don't see it in financial reports these days. For one thing, these assets are not fixed nor permanent, except for land. The assets have several years of usefulness, but they eventually reach the end of their economic lives and are replaced.

The term "fixed" signifies that these assets are not held for sale in the normal course of business, but instead are held for their use in the business. Computers are used for data and word processing, buildings provide the retail, storage, and office space needed in the operations of the business, etc. Capital intensive businesses such as manufacturers, public utilities, hotels, and airlines make heavy investments in long-term, fixed assets. Other companies—many retailers come to mind—do not need to invest very much in fixed assets. Fixed assets are just a fraction of their annual sales.

As you probably know, the cost of fixed assets is spread over their economically useful lives. Well, this is the theory at least.

In practice, the shortest times allowed by the federal income tax law are used to depreciate fixed assets. In other words, depreciation is based more on income tax expediency than on realistic estimates of the expected economic lives of the assets. Airlines fly their jets 15 years, but this doesn't mean they depreciate the cost of their jets over 15 years. The depreciation question is one that managers should be quite clear on since the useful life estimate used to compute the annual depreciation expense causes a large difference in recorded profit for the period.

The main point is that a business has to invest in several different long-term, fixed operating assets. We'll assume that the original cost of these assets was $3,250,000. Many of these fixed assets have been used for one or more years in the past, which means that the assets would have been already depreciated in prior years. This year's $315,000 depreciation expense (see the Income Statement in Table 7–1) is added to the *Accumulated Depreciation* balance carried forward from the previous years' depreciation.

Accumulated Depreciation is a contra account, i.e., a deduction account subtracted from the original cost of the fixed assets. We'll assume that prior to this year $825,000 of depreciation had been recorded on the assets. Thus, this year's $315,000 depreciation is added to the previous balance to give the new balance of $1,140,000. To sum up the depreciation and fixed assets in the Balance Sheet:

$3,250,000 Fixed Assets ↔
                  $ 315,000 Depreciation Expense This Year
                  <u>$ 825,000 </u>Previous Years' Depreciation
                  $1,140,000 Accumulated Depreciation

The Balance Sheet At This Point

Let's take a look at the Balance Sheet up to this point. It's not quite complete, but looking at it here serves to bring out one very critical issue facing managers. Based on the previous discussion of sales revenue and expenses and their related assets and liabilities, the company's Balance Sheet is shown in Table 7–2.

TABLE 7–2
Balance Sheet To This Point

Cash		$ 400,000	
Accounts Receivable		$1,000,000	
Inventory		$1,375,000	
Prepaid Expenses		$ 185,000	
Fixed Assets	$ 3,250,000		
Accumulated Depreciation	$(1,140,000)	$2,110,000	
Total Assets			$5,070,000
Accounts Payable		$ 740,000	
Accrued Expenses		$ 415,000	
Total Liabilities To This Point			$1,155,000
Net Assets (Financed From Debt and Equity Capital Sources)			$3,915,000

The new item in the Balance Sheet is the bottom line, the *net assets* of the business, which is the amount of capital that has to be raised from debt and equity capital sources. The Balance Sheet shows that the business needs to have raised $3,915,000 capital.

Two other expense-based liabilities have not yet been discussed: Accrued Interest Payable for unpaid interest expense and Income Tax Payable for unpaid income tax expense. These two fairly small liabilities would reduce the capital needed by the business, but not very much. The key question at this point is: Where did the business get the capital needed to finance the net assets?

A business has three basic sources of capital: (1) paid-in (invested) capital from equity owners, for example, the stockholders of a corporation; (2) interest-bearing debt; and, (3) retained earnings, which has been discussed earlier in this chapter. This is not a book on business finance, a field which explores the rather large variety of ways to raise capital.

We'll assume stockholders have invested $1,200,000 in past years for which capital stock shares were issued by the corporation. And the business has borrowed $1,500,000 on the basis of short-term and long-term notes payable that bear 10 percent annual interest rate. (The basic choice between debt and equity capital is analyzed in Chapter 9.)

The remainder of net assets (less the relatively small additional liabilities to be added later) is from the accumulated retained earnings of the business. The company has been in business several years, has made a profit most years, and has never paid out dividends equal to its profit any year, so every year some of the profit has been retained in the business.

Again refer to the Income Statement; see Table 7–1. Notice that Interest Expense is $150,000, which is the company's $1,500,000 debt times the 10 percent interest rate. Some parts of this expense may be unpaid at year-end, which is the date at which the Balance Sheet is prepared. Assume that $35,000 of the interest expense has not yet reached its payment date. This accumulated interest expense is recorded in the *Accrued Expenses* account; the $35,000 is added to this liability; which raises its balance to $450,000.

Interest expense is deductible to determine taxable income, as you probably know. Notice in the Income Statement that Earnings Before Income Tax is $1,185,000; this amount is multiplied by the current corporate income tax rate of 34 percent to get the Income Tax Expense of $402,900. In actual practice, determining the income tax would not be as simple as this calculation. But, we'll leave income tax to the CPAs and adopt this straightforward approach.

At year-end (the Balance Sheet date) not all of the income tax expense would have been paid over to Uncle Sam; there would be some amount of unpaid income tax, which we assume is $95,000. Quite naturally, the unpaid amount is found in the *Income Tax Payable* account.

The Completed Balance Sheet And The Nature of Retained Earnings

We now can complete the Balance Sheet as shown in Table 7–3. Notice the $1,085,000 Retained Earnings balance. There are two ways of looking at this amount. First, you could say that it's a "plug" figure, the amount needed to make the Balance Sheet balance. This is not entirely wrong. When liabilities and paid-in capital are subtracted from assets, the remainder has to be the only other source of capital—Retained Earnings. In this sense Re-

TABLE 7–3
Completed Balance Sheet

Cash		$ 400,000	
Accounts Receivable		$1,000,000	
Inventory		$1,375,000	
Prepaid Expenses		$ 185,000	
Fixed Assets	$ 3,250,000		
Accumulated Depreciation	$(1,140,000)	$2,110,000	
Total Assets			$5,070,000
Accounts Payable		$ 740,000	
Accrued Expenses		$ 450,000	
Income Tax Payable		$ 95,000	
Interest-Bearing Debt		$1,500,000	
Capital Stock	$ 1,200,000		
Retained Earnings	$ 1,085,000	$2,285,000	
Total Liabilities & Owner's Equity			$5,070,000

tained Earnings is the residual owners' equity after taking out the amount invested by the owners (the paid-in capital).

The second way of looking at Retained Earnings is the following: It is the cumulative historical balance from adding profit each year to the account and deducting withdrawals of profit paid out to owners. This is true also. As seen earlier in the chapter, profit increases Retained Earnings because the net assets of the business are increased by profit. Withdrawals of profit, such as cash dividends paid to stockholders of a corporation, clearly reduce Retained Earnings.

A LOOK BEHIND AND THE VIEW AHEAD

To be honest, the more interesting chapter is the next one dealing with the Cash Flow Statement. But I don't think you can truly understand the next chapter without first going through the exercise of this chapter. Having a solid grounding in the interactions between the Income Statement and the Balance Sheet is necessary for a good grasp of the Cash Flow Statement.

Managers can let assets get out of control, which means that the assets become too large relative to the sales revenue and expenses of the business. It happens all the time. Accounts Receivable are not collected on time. Inventories become bloated. Fixed assets provide idle capacity. Managers need to lay down control guidelines for every asset, and carefully monitor each asset. When liabilities get out of control they quickly come to the attention of managers; creditors are quick to demand action. But assets can "pile up" without anyone yelling about it. The control of assets is discussed further in Chapter 11.

The next chapter turns to questions on every manager's mind: How much cash flow did profit yield for the year? What were the other sources of cash flow? What uses were made of cash flow? The answer to these questions are essential in reviewing the year just ended, and provide the starting point for planning for next year.

CHAPTER 8

CASH FLOW

Managers often ask: "Why doesn't profit equal cash flow?" "How can I be making profit and have so little cash to show for it at the end of the year?" "What are the main reasons for the difference between cash flow and profit?" "Exactly how much cash flow did profit actually yield for the year?" Or as my CPA son puts it, "If we're in the black, where's the green?" This chapter answers these questions.

We begin the chapter in an unusual manner, one you might not expect. The first thing I would like to show you is the *comparative* Balance Sheet for the company example developed in Chapter 7. The Balance Sheet at the end of the year has already been presented (see Table 7-3).

The company's Income Statement for the year is found on page 110 in the Chapter; we'll refer to it a couple times in this chapter. A quick comment in passing: The business is doing quite well. On net sales of $10 million the company made net income (bottom line profit after interest and income tax) of almost $800 thousand, which is about 8 percent of net sales. (The company's managers must have read this book.)

Presented in Table 8-1 is the *comparative* Balance Sheet for this company which, as you see, reports amounts at the start and end of the year as well as the increase or decrease during the year.[1] The beginning balances for each item at the

---

[1] In their external financial reports to stockholders, most corporations report a three-year comparative Balance Sheet, but do not report the increases/decreases from one year-end to the next. Also, it might be mentioned that the ending balances at the close of one year are the beginning balances at the start of the following year.

TABLE 8–1
Comparative Balance Sheet

	Start of Year	End of Year	Change
Cash	$ 300,000	$ 400,000	$ 100,000
Accounts Receivable	$ 850,000	$ 1,000,000	$ 150,000
Inventory	$1,435,000	$ 1,375,000	$ (60,000)
Prepaid Expenses	$ 162,000	$ 185,000	$ 23,000
Fixed Assets	$2,830,000	$ 3,250,000	$ 420,000
Accumulated Depreciation	$ (825,000)	$(1,140,000)	$(315,000)
Total Assets	$4,752,000	$ 5,070,000	$ 318,000
Accounts Payable	$ 714,000	$ 740,000	$ 26,000
Accrued Expenses	$ 492,000	$ 450,000	$ (42,000)
Income Tax Payable	$ 63,000	$ 95,000	$ 32,000
Interest-Bearing Debt	$1,630,000	$ 1,500,000	$(130,000)
Capital Stock	$1,200,000	$ 1,200,000	$ 0
Retained Earnings	$ 653,000	$ 1,085,000	$ 432,000
Total Liabilities & Owner's Equity	$4,752,000	$ 5,070,000	$ 318,000

start of the year are new; this information has not been presented before.

You might first briefly scan the changes in each asset, each liability, and each owners' equity. Capital stock, for instance, did not change; the company did not issue or retire any of its capital stock shares during the year. All other accounts did change during the year. Cash increased $100,000. One purpose of the Cash Flow Statement is to summarize the causes of this $100,000 Cash increase. Was it due to profit? More debt? Or what?

MANAGEMENT USES OF COMPARATIVE BALANCE SHEET

Although it's something of a well-kept secret, the comparative Balance Sheet is a very useful tool of analysis for managers (and for creditors and external investors, too, for that matter). In particular, the comparative Balance Sheet is the perfect starting point for understanding the Cash Flow Statement (CFS). But it has other important management uses as well.

Cash increased $100,000, as you can see. This increase may have been carefully planned a year ago, or it may simply be the fortuitous result of many decisions and developments during the year that were not guided by any formal plan. Management theory says that cash flows and balances should be closely budgeted and tightly controlled. However, in many companies this is more theory than actual practice. Even if the company does not employ a formal, detailed budget/financial planning system, the manager can use a monthly comparative Balance Sheet to keep reasonably close tabs on changes in the financial condition of the business and the consequences of these changes on Cash.

The manager should keep a sharp eye on the changes in each asset, liability, and owners' equity of the business, and know the reasons for the change. For example, Accounts Receivable increased $150,000, or about 18 percent over the start of the year [$150,000 increase ÷ $850,000 starting balance = about 18%]. Did sales revenue increase 18 percent over last year? Or was the Accounts Receivable increase due to longer credit terms offered to customers? Perhaps there is a much larger amount of past-due receivables at the end of the year which would raise questions about their collectibility. The manager can't guess at these reasons. The manager must know why.

In contrast to Accounts Receivables, Inventories decreased $60,000. Is this good or bad? Normally less inventory is better, all other things being equal, because of the high costs of carrying inventory. Annual carrying (holding) costs add 20/30 percent or more to the purchase (or manufacturing) cost of inventory. The inventory decrease could be due to stock-outs of high-demand products that caused lost sales during the year. These questions must be answered.

These and other management control uses of the comparative Balance Sheet are discussed further in Chapter 11. This chapter is concerned with cash flows, and how the Cash Flow Statement and the comparative Balance Sheet are like two sets of puzzle pieces that fit together to give the whole picture of the financial affairs of the business.

THE CASH FLOW STATEMENT

From one viewpoint the Cash Flow Statement (CFS) is an explanation of the changes column in the comparative Balance Sheet. This may sound odd. You may think that the CFS summarizes the basic sources and uses of cash during the year, which is true. However, don't forget that for every change in Cash there is an equal amount of change in another asset, or liability, or owners' equity. There are no exceptions. The basic reciprocal relationship between cash and the other components of financial condition is the anchor point for understanding cash flow.

The basic rules of cash flow are simple. An increase in an asset is a negative cash flow, and an increase in a liability or owners' equity is a positive cash flow. Conversely, a decrease in an asset is a positive cash flow, and a decrease in a liability or owners' equity is a negative cash flow. (See Table 8-2).

In other words, cash flow is opposite to changes in assets and in the same direction as changes in liabilities and owners' equity. You increase cash flow by decreasing assets or by increasing liabilities and owners' equity. And vice versa. With this in mind, let's take a look at the CFS.

Introducing the Cash Flow Statement (CFS)

Exhibit 8-1 shows the *Cash Flow Statement* for the company, including "lines of connection" and match-ups with the changes column from the comparative Balance Sheet (see page 125). The seven Balance Sheet accounts in the two "boxes" match up with the same seven items in the boxed area in the Cash Flow Statement.

TABLE 8–2
Basic Cash Flow Effects

	Increase	Decrease
ASSET	− Cash Flow	+ Cash Flow
LIABILITY or OWNER'S EQUITY	+ Cash Flow	− Cash Flow

You may be surprised to know that the Cash Flow Statement (CFS) is a very recent addition to external financial reports. The Financial Accounting Standards Board, the rule-making body for generally accepted accounting principles that govern external financial reporting by businesses, issued the official pronouncement for the CFS in late 1987.

Many corporations had been reporting a cash flow statement under a previous ruling that became effective in 1971. However, under this earlier ruling corporations had the option to report a funds flow statement instead of a cash flow statement, and many did. The main purpose of the 1987 ruling was to make the cash flow statement mandatory, and to standardize the basic classifications in the statement as well as its format.

The amazing thing is that it took so long for the Cash Flow Statement to be made mandatory. Security analysts had long requested this information. Good managers have long realized the importance of analyzing cash flows. In any case, the statement is now required for all profit-motivated businesses, large and small.

Our interest in the Cash Flow Statement, and let me make this very clear, is from the *manager's* point of view. The basic thrust of the external financial reporting standard is in harmony with the management approach. However, the pronouncement was written as an authoritative guide for external financial reporting, not from the manager's point of view.

I am mainly concerned with making things clear to managers. For instance, the lines of connection and match-ups shown in Exhibit 8-1 are not shown in external financial reports, as you would surmise. Few corporations report the amounts of changes in their comparative Balance Sheets. This is unacceptable for internal management reporting. Can you imagine asking a high-level manager, say Lee Iacocca, the President of Chrysler, to get out a calculator and make all these calculations? Managers can and should ask for as much detailed information as they need, whereas, external financial statements report information at a very summary level.[2]

---

[2] For instance, in the external CFS, cash can be grouped with "cash equivalents" and only the sum needed be reported. Cash equivalents include short-term, liquid invest-

EXHIBIT 8–1

Changes from Comparative Balance Sheet

Cash	$100,000
Accounts Receivable	$150,000
Inventory	($60,000)
Prepaid Expenses	$23,000
Fixed Assets	$420,000
Accumulated Depreciation	($315,000)
Accounts Payable	$26,000
Accrued Expenses	($42,000)
Income Tax Payable	$32,000
Interest Bearing Debt	($130,000)
Capital Stock	$0
Retained Earnings	$432,000

Cash Flow Statement

Cash Flow from Operations (Profit)

Net Income	$782,100
Accounts Receivable Increase	($150,000)
Inventory Decrease	$60,000
Prepaid Expenses Increase	($23,000)
Depreciation Expense	$315,000
Accounts Payable Increase	$26,000
Accrued Expenses Decrease	($42,000)
Income Tax Payable Increase	$32,000
	$1,000,100

Cash Flows of Financing Transactions

Debt Borrowing	$250,000
Debt Payments	($380,000)
Cash Dividends	($350,100)
	($480,100)

Cash Flows of Investing Transactions

Purchase of New Fixed Assets	($420,000)
Net Increase of Cash During Year	$100,000

The Three Parts of the Cash Flow Statement (CFS)

The CFS is divided into three parts: (1) cash flow from *profit* (operations); (2) cash flow from *financing*; and, (3) cash flow from *investing*.[3] The second and third parts are straightforward.

Financing refers to the borrowing and repaying of debt as well as the issuing and retiring of equity securities (common and preferred stock). Basically, this part of the CFS summarizes the transactions of the business during the year with its external sources of capital, in other words, its debt and equity sources.

Please refer again to Exhibit 8-1. The business borrowed $250,000 during the year and repaid $380,000 of its debt for a net decrease, or "pay-down," of $130,000. This decreases Cash. There is also another financing transaction during the year; the company paid $350,100 cash dividends to its stockholders.

Cash dividends are classified or treated as a financing transaction in the CFS because dividends are "payment" for the use of equity capital. That is, cash dividends are part of the "contract" with its capital stockholders. The Board of Directors have to meet and make a formal decision regarding how much cash dividends, if any, should be paid to the stockholders. One factor that influences their decision is the cash flow from profit, which we'll turn to shortly.

The total cash *outflow* from the company's financing transactions during the year is $480,100, as you can see in the CFS. Nevertheless, the company purchased new fixed assets, which leads to the third section of the CFS.

Investing refers to capital expenditures, i.e., investments in long-lived, fixed assets, which includes land, buildings, machinery, equipment, vehicles, tools, and so on. Notice that the company spent $420,000 to purchase new fixed assets during the

---

ments that can be immediately converted into definite amounts of cash and which are so close to their maturities that the market fluctuation risk is virtually nil. The prime example is U.S. Government Treasury Bills.

[3] In external financial reports, the preferred order is to put investing before financing cash flows. However, from the management viewpoint I think it makes more sense to put financing ahead of investing.

year, which decreases Cash. This part of the CFS would include cash inflows from any divestments of long-lived assets, i.e., cash receipts from disposals of such assets. In this example the business did not dispose of any fixed assets, so there is no cash inflow from this source.

Many companies have a variety of long-term assets, not just fixed assets used in the operations of the business. Often there is a fair amount of turnover in these investments during the year; the Investing section of the CFS gets rather "messy" for these companies, especially larger diversified conglomerates that have a broad range of investments.

Cash Flow From Profit (Operations)

How much cash flow did the company realize from its net income (profit) during the year? Managers should be certain to know the answer to this key question.

As a general rule, cash flow does **not** equal profit; this would be extremely rare. Cash flow is either more or less than profit, and the amount of difference can be quite large. In this example, cash flow from profit is $1,000,100, which is $218,000 more than profit for the year (see the CFS in Exhibit 8-1). In other years it may be less than profit for the year. It can even be negative, that is, profit might cause a decrease in cash during the year!

A company may experience negative cash flow even though it makes a profit for the year. And it may have positive cash flow for the year even though it suffers a loss. It all depends on the changes in the operating assets and operating liabilities that are an integral and inseparable part of sales revenue and expenses. Each of these is examined in turn, starting with Accounts Receivable.

Accounts Receivable

Accounts Receivable increased $150,000 during the year; the ending balance is $150,000 more than the balance at the start of the year. This is bad news from the cash flow point of view, though it may be good news from the marketing point of view if the increase is due to sales growth. The Accounts Receivable increase is analyzed in Table 8-3.

TABLE 8-3
Cash Flow From Sales Revenue During Year

Net Sales	$10,000,000
Accounts Receivable at End of Year	(1,000,000)
Cash Collected from This Year's Sales	$ 9,000,000
Accounts Receivable at Start of Year	850,000
Cash Collected From Customers During Year	$ 9,850,000

Net Sales were $10,000,000 for the year. However, at the end of the year there was $1,000,000 uncollected sales revenue, which is the balance in ending Accounts Receivable. So, only $9,000,000 of this year's sales revenue was collected in Cash during the year. However, the company collected the $850,000 beginning balance of Accounts Receivable. Basically, the ending balance hurts cash flow and the beginning balance helps cash flow. The net effect is a negative $150,000; cash collected from customers is only $9,850,000, which is $150,000 less than the net sales of $10,000,000.

One alternative method of presenting Cash Flow From Profit (Operations) is to report cash flows in this manner, i.e., the Income Statement would be recast into cash flow amounts for each revenue and expense. So, $10,000,000 Net Sales Revenue would be replaced with $9,850,000 Cash Collected From Customers. Each Income Statement item would be translated into its cash flow amount for the year. In fact, this alternative is preferred by the Financial Accounting Standards Board. Personally, I don't agree. The Income Statement is the natural center of gravity for managers, and an alternative "cash flow" version of the Income Statement would only add confusion in my opinion.

The cash flow calculation isn't too bad for Sales Revenue, but it gets much more complex for many expenses. I don't think many companies will elect this option in their external financial reports or for internal management uses. They will report cash flow from profit in the manner shown in Exhibit 8-1.

As you can see there, the CFS starts with net income from the bottom line of the Income Statement, and then cash flow adjustments are made to get to the cash flow from profit. As just mentioned, from the management viewpoint I definitely prefer this approach. For one thing, it ties in directly with the comparative Balance Sheet and, thus, leaves a clear trail to follow. Managers use the comparative Balance Sheet as a basic financial control tool, so it makes sense to get double mileage out of it and tie it with the Cash Flow Statement as well.

Inventory

Inventory decreased $60,000 during the year, which is not a large change compared to its $1,435,000 beginning balance. The Inventory change is a positive cash flow factor; notice that the $60,000 is added to Net Income, whereas, the $150,000 Accounts Receivable increase is subtracted (see Exhibit 8-1 again). The basic explanation of the positive cash flow impact of the Inventory decrease is explained in Table 8-4.

The cost of inventory is charged to Cost of Goods Sold Expense as the products are sold to customers. This expense is $6,250,000 for the year (see the Income Statement in Table 7-1). The company started the year with $1,435,000 Inventory; this much was already on hand and did not have to be purchased during the year. So, the beginning amount of Inventory is subtracted from the expense. However, the company replaces inventory as sold and had $1,375,000 cost invested in Inventory at the end of the year. Ending Inventory is added to determine cash paid out for inventory during the year.

Notice that the cash outflow for inventory is $6,190,000, which is $60,000 less than the Cost of Goods Sold Expense of $6,250,000. Basically the company "liquidated" $60,000 of inventory; it didn't replace all its beginning inventory. Thus, the company avoided $60,000 cash outlay, which is a positive cash factor. If the company had ended the year with zero inventory, for an extreme example, it would have had to spend only

TABLE 8–4
Cash Flow Of Cost of Goods Sold Expense

Cost of Goods Sold Expense	$6,250,000
Inventory at Start of Year	(1,435,000)
Cash Paid For Inventory Sold This Year	$4,815,000
Inventory at End of Year	1,375,000
Cash Paid For Inventory During Year	$6,190,000

$4,815,000 on the products sold during the year, being the cost of those goods sold during the year that were not on hand at the start of the year.

One thing wrong with the above analysis is that it fails to recognize that inventory is bought on credit. We should also take into account the Accounts Payable amounts at the start and end of the year that were for inventory purchases. This is one case from several that makes cash flow analysis of expenses more complex than cash flow analysis sales revenue where you only have to consider Accounts Receivable.[4]

Frankly, I don't think the effort is worth it. Managers should know the basics, but beyond this leave it to the accountants. The basic point is that an increase in an operating asset (one directly tied with sales revenue or an expense) causes a negative cash flow impact. An operating asset decrease causes a positive cash flow impact.

Prepaid Expenses

Prepaid Expenses increased $23,000 during the year, which is a negative cash flow (see Exhibit 8-1 again). During the year the company "used up" all of its beginning balance of these prepaid operating costs and replaced them with an even larger amount at the end of the year. So, the increase of this operating asset was an additional demand on cash flow for the year, though not a very large one.

Depreciation–Care Required

The next item is much larger–the $315,000 depreciation expense for the year. In this example, the business did not dispose any of its depreciable assets during the year. Every asset at the start of the year is still on hand and in use at the end of the year. I mention this again because it means that all of the increase in Accumulated Depreciation is equal to depreciation expense for the year.

---

[4] A company may collect sales revenue in advance and, thus, have an Unearned Revenue liability account to bring into the analysis, in addition to Accounts Receivable.

In many situations there are disposals of fixed assets during the year. The accumulated depreciation on the assets disposed of would have been removed from Accumulated Depreciation. In this case, the change in Accumulated Depreciation would be the increase from depreciation expense for the year less the amount removed for assets disposed of. The point is that the Accumulated Depreciation account does not always increase by the amount of the depreciation expense for the year. The more important point is that managers need to be very clear about depreciation and cash flow from profit.

Depreciation expense follows the general rule. Depreciation expense decreases the fixed assets of the business by increasing the Accumulated Depreciation deduction from the original cost of the fixed assets. A decrease in an operating asset is a positive cash flow factor.

As with the decrease of Inventory, depreciation is "added back" to net income to determine cash flow from profit. Depreciation expense is not a cash outflow; the company did not write a check for its depreciation. The assets being depreciated, at least the large majority of them, were bought and paid for in past years. (Notice, however, that the company did purchase $420,000 of new fixed assets during the year and some depreciation expense was recorded on these new assets.)

Often persons who should know better say that depreciation and only depreciation should be "added back" to net income to determine cash flow from profit. This is definitely incorrect and can be very misleading. They also say that depreciation "is only a book entry," implying that it's not really an expense or suggesting that depreciation expense is a rather arbitrary amount that depends on what useful life is adopted for the assets, and what method of depreciation is elected. The same things can be said about inventory and cost of goods sold expense. There is more than one method of inventory accounting to determine the cost of goods sold expense for the year; furthermore, inventory write-downs usually have to be made, and these charges are arbitrary.

The main lesson is that the manager must look at **all** the changes in operating assets and liabilities during the year, and not become myopic about depreciation. Even professional financial analysts often take a unwise short-cut and simply add back depreciation to net income and call the total cash flow from profit. This ignores the several other items that can have an even bigger impact on cash flow from profit.

I must admit that in this example depreciation is the largest cash flow factor; accounts receivable is a distant second. In other situations there may be much larger changes than depreciation, or the other items collected together may have negative cash flow effects which offset the positive depreciation factor.

The Three Operating Liabilities

Next we turn to the three operating liabilities that impact on the cash flow from profit. The general rule is this: Increases in these liabilities increase cash flow from profit, and decreases in these liabilities decrease cash flow. Consider Accounts Payable, the first of the three operating liabilities.

As discussed in Chapter 7, inventory, as well as many expenses, is bought on credit. The balance of Accounts Payable is the sum of unpaid inventory purchases and unpaid expenses. Until paid, there is no cash outflow. At year-end there was $740,000 Accounts Payable not yet paid. At the start of the year there was $714,000 Accounts Payable which was paid during the year. The ending "unpaids" are $26,000 larger than the beginning "paids." The net cash flow impact is a positive $26,000, which is added back to net income as you can see in the Exhibit 8-1.

There are two other operating liabilities: one decreased and one increased. The Accrued Expenses liability is explained in Chapter 7. The $450,000 of Accrued Expenses at the end of the year is the amount of unpaid expenses that have been recorded in this account, which is in addition to unpaid expenses recorded in Accounts Payable. Until these are paid next year, there is no drain on cash. However, the $492,000 of Accrued Expenses at the start of the year was paid during the year. The difference between the two amounts is a net decrease of $42,000, which is negative cash flow factor on profit.

Income Tax Payable was $95,000 at the end of the year compared with $63,000 at the start of the year. The beginning amount was paid, but the ending amount was not. So, the net cash flow impact is a positive $32,000. In other words, the cash outlay during the year for income tax was $32,000 less than the expense for the year.

Finally—Cash Flow From Profit (Operations)
Taking into account the several changes in operating assets and liabilities, cash flow from profit was $1,000,100 for the year as reported in the CFS (see Exhibit 8-1 again). In summary, cash flow is $218,000 more than profit, a nice situation to be in. As the CFS reports, cash flow from profit provided enough to pay cash dividends, pay down debt, buy new fixed assets, and even provide a modest increase in Cash.

Things don't always go so well, of course. Next, we take a second look at the same company, but for a different example in which its cash flow from profit is much less than profit. In fact, cash flow from profit is **zero** even though it earned a very healthy profit (net income) of $782,100 for the year. How do you like that?

ZERO CASH FLOW FROM PROFIT

In this new example the Balance Sheet of the company at the end of the year is exactly the same as before, but at the start of the year things were much different. I want to show you an example of zero cash flow from profit. So I've made every change in operating assets and operating liabilities the "wrong way," to cause a negative impact on cash flow (except that depreciation expense is still a positive cash flow factor of course).

The comparative Balance Sheet of the company for this new example is shown in Table 8-5.

Notice the many changes in the Balance Sheet at the start of the year and the very different amounts in the changes column for most of the items. Since the company had zero cash flow from profit, its Board of Directors decided not to pay any cash dividends to stockholders during the year. Thus, notice that the increase in Retained Earnings is equal to the profit for the year or $782,100.

Interest-bearing debt was reduced $130,000, the same as before, and $420,000 of new fixed assets were purchased, the

TABLE 8-5
Comparative Balance Sheet for Zero Cash Flow Example

	Start of Year	End of Year	Change
Cash	$ 950,000	$ 400,000	$(550,000)
Accounts Receivable	$ 750,000	$ 1,000,000	$ 250,000
Inventory	$ 940,900	$ 1,375,000	$ 434,100
Prepaid Expenses	$ 92,000	$ 185,000	$ 93,000
Fixed Assets	$ 2,830,000	$ 3,250,000	$ 420,000
Accumulated Depreciation	$ (825,000)	$(1,140,000)	$(315,000)
Total Assets	$ 4,737,900	$ 5,070,000	$ 332,100
Accounts Payable	$ 900,000	$ 740,000	$(160,000)
Accrued Expenses	$ 590,000	$ 450,000	$(140,000)
Income Tax Payable	$ 115,000	$ 95,000	$ (20,000)
Interest Bearing Debt	$ 1,630,000	$ 1,500,000	$(130,000)
Capital Stock	$ 1,200,000	$ 1,200,000	$ 0
Retained Earnings	$ 302,900	$ 1,085,000	$ 782,100
Total Liabilities & Owner's Equity	$ 4,737,900	$ 5,070,000	$ 332,100

same as before. Thus, interest expense and depreciation expense are the same as before.

In short, the Income Statement for this new example is exactly the same. The biggest difference is that cash flow from profit is exactly zero, as shown in Table 8-6.

In contrast to before, no lines of connection are shown between the CFS and the comparative Balance Sheet. The CFS is shown "naked" by itself. This is deliberate. You should be able to cross-tie the amounts in the two statements.

Cash flow from profit is zero. Therefore, the $130,000 paydown on debt plus the $420,000 purchase of new fixed assets reduced the Cash balance by $550,000, as you can see in both the CFS and comparative Balance Sheet. Fortunately, the company had a large enough Cash balance at the start of the year to permit this, although as mentioned before, no cash dividends were paid to stockholders during the year. Recall from the earlier example that $350,100 cash dividends were paid. So, the debt reduction and new fixed assets were at the expense of any cash dividends, which may not please the stockholders.

TABLE 8-6
Cash Flow Statement

Cash Flow From Operations (Profit)

Net Income	$ 782,100	
Accounts Receivable Increase	$(250,000)	
Inventory Increase	$(434,100)	
Prepaid Expenses Increase	$ (93,000)	
Depreciation Expense	$ 315,000	
Accounts Payable Decrease	$(160,000)	
Accrued Expenses Decrease	$(140,000)	
Income Tax-Payable Decrease	$ (20,000)	$ 0

Cash Flows of Financing Transactions

Debt Borrowing	$ 250,000	
Debt Payments	$(380,000)	
Cash Dividends	$ 0	
		$(130,000)

Cash Flows of Investing Transactions

Purchase of New Fixed Assets	$(420,000)
Net Decrease of Cash During Year	$(550,000)

SUMMARY OF CASH FLOW FROM PROFIT

The Basic Formula For Cash Flow From Profit

Seldom is profit equal to cash flow; cash flow is almost always more or less than profit. Changes in operating assets and operating liabilities help or hurt cash flow, and these almost always change. Also, there is depreciation. To summarize, see Table 8-7.

Managers must understand the impacts of changes in operating assets and liabilities on cash flow. These cash flow impacts are precisely why managers need to control changes in their operating assets and liabilities. The manager carefully has to monitor changes in operating assets and operating liabilities to keep tabs on cash flow from profit.

TABLE 8–7
Cash Flow From Profit

Net Income
+ Depreciation (and Amortization and Depletion, if any)
− Increase in Operating Assets
+ Decreases in Operating Assets
− Decreases in Operating Liabilities
+ Increases in Operating Liabilities
= Cash Flow From Profit (Operations)

Refer once again to the comparative Balance Sheet (see Table 8-5). The manager should be very concerned why Accounts Receivable increased $250,000 or one-third over the start of the year. Likewise, why did Inventory increase more than $400 thousand, and why did Prepaid Expenses more than double? Continuing down to operating liabilities, why did the business pay down its Accounts Payable by $160,000, and its Accrued Expenses by $140,000? And, why did Income Tax Payable decrease $20,000? All these changes put heavy strains on cash flow.

In short, you control cash flow from profit by controlling the operating assets and operating liabilities that determine cash flow. Much depends on the trend of sales revenue. Sales growth demands increases in operating assets with corresponding increases in operating liabilities. Sales declines should lead to declines in operating assets and liabilities.

Sales Trends and Cash Flow From Profit

Cash flow from profit is a very telling number. It draws attention to the changes in operating assets and liabilities and raises the obvious question of whether the managers have these changes under control. The benchmark is the sales revenue trend line of the business, as just mentioned. What's good for sales is bad for cash flow, and conversely, what's bad for sales is good for cash flow.

Sales growth hurts cash flow from profit. Operating assets increase in more or less the same proportion as sales growth. For instance, if sales revenue increases 30 percent then, as a rough rule of thumb, Accounts Receivable and Inventory tend to increase about 30 percent. On the other side of the coin, operating liabilities also increase, which partially offsets the damage done by increases in operating assets.

High growth rates can cause negative cash flow from profit. In these explosive sales-growth situations, it's not unusual that large increases in operating assets less the increases in operating liabilities is an amount that is more than net income plus depreciation.

In the reverse direction, it's ironic that a sales decline helps cash flow from profit. A decrease in sales revenue means that operating assets should decrease at more or less the same rate, although oftentimes managers are reluctant to downsize Inventory. Operating liabilities also decrease as sales revenue decreases, which partially offsets cash flow benefit from the decreases in operating assets.

A Final Word

The essence of good financial planning is to start with a good sales forecast for the coming year. Forecast sales for next year are then compared with actual sales revenue for the year just ended. Based on the budgeted increase or decrease in sales revenue, the manager then should determine the appropriate amounts of increases or decreases in the operating assets and liabilities for the coming year. Once these changes have been budgeted, cash flow from profit next year can be determined, which is the essential starting point for planning the financing and investing plans of the business for the coming year.

The higher the cash flow from profit, the more money there is for cash dividends and investing, and less money will have to be raised from debt and equity financing. The lower the cash flow from profit, the less money there is for cash dividends and investing, and more money will have to be raised from debt and equity financing.

The critical importance of controlling changes in operating assets and liabilities is clear. These changes determine the cash flow from profit, which, in turn, determines the basic financial course of the business. Without enough cash flow from profit, dividends may have to be eliminated or reduced drastically, investing may have to be curtailed, and the business may be forced into high cost financing alternatives. A strong cash flow from profit provides the money for paying cash dividends, and is a ready pool of capital for expanding the business and realigning its debt and equity mix to a more favorable advantage. In short, cash flow from profit is the lifeline of any business.

CHAPTER 9

RETURN ON CAPITAL

ASSETS AND CAPITAL SOURCES

Several different *operating* assets and *operating* liabilities are needed to carry on profit-making activities, as Chapter 7 explains. These assets and liabilities are the preconditions (the "before") and the results (the "after") of revenues and expenses.

To review briefly: Making sales on credit generates *Accounts Receivable*; selling products requires *Inventory* and buying products on credit results in *Accounts Payable*; operating expenses require *Prepaid Expenses* and also result in *Accounts Payable* and *Accrued Expenses*. A business also needs a certain amount of *Cash* as a buffer or safety margin against fluctuations in cash flow from day to day, week to week, and month to month. And, businesses need long-term operating assets: land, buildings, equipment, vehicles, machinery, furniture, computers, and so on.[1]

Operating assets don't earn interest income and operating liabilities don't require interest expense, though there are exceptions. Excess Cash balances may be invested temporarily in highly liquid, safe securities (such as short-term U.S. Government issues) to earn interest income on surplus Cash instead of letting it lie idle. Customers who delay too long in paying their receivables may be charged interest beyond the normal credit period. Likewise, if the business delays too long in paying its

---

[1]Instead of buying its long-term assets, a business may lease them, which is examined in the next chapter.

accounts payable, it may be charged interest beyond the normal credit period. Putting aside these minor exceptions, operating assets don't earn interest income and operating liabilities don't bear interest expense.

Operating assets less operating liabilities is the total amount of *capital* the business must raise. Broadly speaking, the business has two sources of capital—*debt* and *equity*. (Equity includes both paid-in capital and retained earnings.) I assume that you know the basic nature of debt and equity and the differences between each source of capital, and that you are aware of the many variations and different features of debt and equity instruments. Just a few quick comments are made here.

Debt may be secured with collateral, or not; it may be very short-term (six months or less) or very long-term (twenty years or more). It may be very restrictive or it may be quite liberal and nonbinding on the business. Debt may be convertible into equity stock shares, or not. Equity capital may be supplied by just one person who operates the business as a sole proprietor; i.e., the business may not be organized as a separate legal entity. Or, the business may be a partnership of two or more persons.

Most businesses, even relatively small ones, are organized as corporations, which are legal entities separate from their owners. There are actually millions of corporations in the American economy. Corporations issue stock shares, which are the units of equity ownership in the corporation. A corporation may issue only one class of stock shares, called common stock or capital stock. Or, a corporation may issue both preferred and common stock shares. Now let me quickly say here that this is not a book on business finance.

The many variations and alternatives for financing the capital needs of business are beyond the scope of this book. Many excellent books are available. This chapter examines the basic choice between debt and equity. Debt obviously bears an explicit and legally contracted rate of interest. Equity capital does not.[2]

---

[2]Preferred stock shares carry a stated rate of cash dividend, but payment of the annual dividend is contingent on the corporation earning enough net income and having enough cash on hand to pay the dividend.

But equity capital has an imputed or implicit cost. The business must earn a satisfactory rate of earnings on its equity to justify the use of this capital. Failure to do so reduces the value of the equity and makes it more difficult to attract additional equity capital (if and when needed). Equity capital assumes the risk of business failure and poor performance, but has no limits on its participation in the success of the business.

COMPLETING THE PROFIT PROFILE AND PROFILES OF ASSETS INVESTMENT AND CAPITAL SOURCES

Setting The Stage

Three profiles are shown in Exhibit 9–1 for CAPCO—for profit, for assets investment, and for capital sources. However, the profiles are incomplete at this point. The Profit Profile supresses all information between Sales Revenue and Operating Profit, not because it's unimportant, but because we have already discussed this broad range of topics in the first six chapters.

This chapter focuses on what's below the operating profit line. As you can see, this information is not yet entered in the Profit Profile. Interest expense depends on how much debt is

EXHIBIT 9–1
Profiles of Profit, Assets Investment, & Capital Sources

Assets Investment Profile		Profit Profile	
Operating Assets	$ 1,400,000	Sales Revenue	$2,000,000
Operating Liabilities	$ (400,000)	•	•
Assets Investment	$ 1,000,000	•	•
		•	•
		•	•
Capital Sources Profile		•	•
		Operating Profit	$ 160,000
		Interest Expense	???????????
Debt	??????????	Taxable Income	???????????
Equity	??????????	Income Tax Expense	???????????
Total Capital	$1,000,000	Net Income	???????????

used and, of course, the rate of interest on the debt. Interest is deductible for income tax, so the income tax expense is not entered either. Thus, bottom line net income is not entered.

The totals of operating assets and operating liabilities are entered in the Assets Investment Profile, but not the individual assets and liabilities making up these totals. The several types of operating assets and operating liabilities of a business are examined in Chapter 7. Notice that CAPCO needs to raise $1,000,000 capital, which is its total assets investment or net of operating liabilities. The mix of debt and equity capital sources is not yet entered in the Capital Sources Profile. Alternative mixes of debt and equity are analyzed in the following discussion.

No Debt/All Equity: Conservative But Wise?

You might be surprised how many businesses are anti-debt; they avoid debt like the plague. Other than trade credit (accounts payable) and accrued expenses, these businesses have no liabilities; they don't borrow money. Or at most, they borrow only to bridge over short-term seasonal needs. Their long-term capital is all equity—amounts paid in by stockholders plus accumulated retained earnings. Their stockholders provided enough capital to get the business started and infused additional capital if and when it was needed. Most of these businesses make good profit and generate good cash flow from operations; without this internal source of capital they would have been forced to borrow along the way.

Some years ago I was talking with the Controller of such a company. He was in the middle of designing a new cost accounting system for the company. I naturally assumed this was being done to update the company's accounting system and to improve control reports to managers. But no, the main reason had to do with the company's anti-debt policy.

The company had decided to start up production of a new product, one that has in fact become very successful I might add. The company had prepared a pro-forma (projected) profile of the operating assets and liabilities for the new product (such as developed in Chapter 7). Several million dollars of additional capital would be needed—beyond the resources of the brothers who owned all the company's stock shares. Given the excellent reputation of the company and the fact it virtually had no debt outstanding, banks were standing in line to loan money to them.

However, the brothers were so opposed to debt that they instructed the Controller to identify the products with the lowest profit margins so they could drop one or more of these products to make room for the new product. It turned out that all the present products were too profitable to abandon. So, the brothers broke with their traditional policy, borrowed money, started up the new product, and did very well, although they never got used to the idea of being accountable to the banks, and they hated negotiating renewal of the loans.

In any case, the no-debt alternative is a useful point of reference. The only other factor we need to know is the income tax rate. The following analysis uses the maximum corporate tax rate under the Tax Reform Act (TRA) of 1986, which is 34 percent. This is a conservative approach, which will be discussed in more detail later. The three profiles are now completed and shown in Exhibit 9–2.

Interest Expense is zero, of course, so taxable income equals operating profit. Income tax takes away 34 percent or $54,400, leaving $105,600 net income.[3]

The company's *Return on Equity (ROE)* is computed as follows:

$105,600 Net Income ÷ $1,000,000 Equity = 10.56% ROE

Return on Equity (ROE) is the fundamental measure used by investors to judge or assess earnings on equity capital. The word *return* means earnings, in this case bottom line net income. ROE is 10.56 percent for the year, which is not too bad, but not all that great either. This comment raises the larger question regarding which benchmark or reference should be the basis of comparison. It's the old question, "Relative to what?"

---

[3]A technical point: Adding Income Tax Expense in the Profit Profile means that total Operating Liabilities should be increased slightly in the Assets Investment Profile. Not all of the Income Tax Expense would be paid out in cash during the year; there would be some Income Tax Payable at year-end, which is an Operating Liability. However, this relatively minor adjustment is not made to keep the example easier to follow.

EXHIBIT 9-2
No Debt/All Equity Capital Mix

Assets Investment Profile		Profit Profile	
Operating Assets	$1,400,000	Sales Revenue	$2,000,000
Operating Liabilities	$ (400,000)	•	•
Assets Investment	$1,000,000	•	•
		•	•
Capital Sources Profile		•	•
		Operating Profit	$ 160,000
		Interest Expense	$ 0
Debt	$0	Taxable Income	$ 160,000
Equity	$1,000,000	Income Tax Expense	$ (54,400)
Total Capital	$1,000,000	Net Income	$ 105,600

The basic idea is that the $1,000,000 invested in the business could have been invested somewhere else and earned return (earnings) from the alternative investment. But precisely what rate of return? Should ROE be compared with a riskless and highly liquid investment, such as short-term U.S. Government securities? Probably not. ROE should be compared with a comparable investment that has about the same risk and liquidity. The appropriate earnings rate on the "other" or next best investment is called the *opportunity cost of capital*. To avoid the argument over the most appropriate benchmark, we'll simply assume the stockholders would like to do better, which implies that their opportunity cost of capital is higher than the 10.56 percent ROE earned by CAPCO.

Heavy Debt/Light Equity: High Financial Leverage

Let's go from one extreme to the other—from no debt in the previous scenario to very heavy debt. There's a limit to how much debt a business can borrow, though this depends on how far lenders are willing to go. To dramatize the example, we'll assume a very heavy debt load, which realistically is probably more than the average business could borrow. Using debt instead of or to supplement equity capital is referred to as *financial leverage*. The term also refers to using debt to improve ROE, as is examined next.

The basic strategy of financial leverage is fairly straightforward. To begin, notice CAPCO's rate of Operating Profit on Assets Investment:

$$\$160{,}000 \text{ Operating Profit} \div \$1{,}000{,}000 \text{ Assets Investment} = 16.0\%$$

The business earns a pre-interest, pre-tax 16.0 percent rate of return on its assets investment. In other words, its EBIT (earnings before interest and tax) is 16.0 percent of its net operating assets (operating assets less operating liabilities).

There's no one standard or universal term for this particular rate of return, even though it's extremely important. It's not completely accurate to call it the *Return on Assets*, though this term is often used. For one thing, the term "return" doesn't make it clear that it means operating profit before interest and income tax. For another thing, the term "assets" implies total assets before deducting operating liabilities. However, it's the most commonly used term, so we'll use it. So, the business earns 16.0 percent *ROA* (return on assets). Please keep in mind the precise meaning of the term as we proceed.

Suppose CAPCO can borrow money at an annual interest rate less than its 16.0 percent ROA. Thus, it can substitute debt for equity capital and thereby increase its ROE (return on equity). Assume, for example, the business can borrow money at an annual interest rate of 10.0 percent, which is six points less than its ROA. This favorable "spread" between the two rates generates a leverage gain or improvement in the ROE. The spread is the key point. On each dollar borrowed the business earns 16 cents but pays only 10 cents interest, so it is 6 cents ahead (before income tax is considered).

The impact of financial leverage is best seen in the following example. Assume the business has borrowed $750,000 at an annual interest rate of 10.0 percent, and thus needs only $250,000 equity capital. This is a very heavy debt load, as mentioned before. It might very well be more than the "debt capacity" of the business, which is the theoretical maximum debt load the business could handle without serious risk of default (given its earnings and cash flow prospects). The three profiles for this situation are as shown in Exhibit 9–3.

Net income drops to $56,100. But notice what happens to ROE:

$$\$56,100 \text{ Net Income} \div \$250,000 \text{ Equity Capital} = 22.44\% \text{ ROE}$$

The company's ROE more than doubles compared with the previous no-debt situation in which ROE was just over 10.0 percent. Of course, the 22 percent ROE applies only on the $250,000 equity capital invested in the business. A complete investment analysis comparing the alternative debt and capital mixes should also consider the other $750,000 of equity capital that is no longer invested in the business (the amount displaced by debt). Although the stockholders may have had only $250,000 to invest in the first place, in which case there would be no equity displacement.

To some extent, comparing different debt/equity mixes is comparing apples and oranges. Equity capital not invested in the business is invested somewhere else, but the "somewhere else" is bound to be a different type of investment, one not fully comparable with the risk and liquidity factors of investing in the business. This issue takes us into the fields of business fi-

EXHIBIT 9–3
Heavy Debt/Light Equity Capital Mix

Assets Investment Profile		Profit Profile	
Operating Assets	$1,400,000	Sales Revenue	$2,000,000
Operating Liabilities	$ (400,000)	•	•
Assets Investment	$1,000,000	•	•
		•	•
Capital Sources Profile		•	•
		Operating Profit	$ 160,000
		Interest Expense	$ (75,000)
Debt (at 10.0%)	$ 750,000	Taxable Income	$ 85,000
Equity	$ 250,000	Income Tax Expense	$ (28,900)
Total Capital	$1,000,000	Net Income	$ 56,100

nance and investments, which are beyond the scope of this book. The objective here is to show the basic impact of financial leverage on ROE.

One other scenario is worth a quick look, for example, when the interest rate is the same as the company's ROA. If CAPCO's annual interest rate had been 16.0 percent, its profiles would appear as shown in Exhibit 9–4.

Notice that ROE in this situation is the same as in the previous no debt/all equity situation:

$$\$26{,}400 \text{ Net Income} \div \$250{,}000 \text{ Equity Capital}$$
$$= 10.56\% \text{ ROE}$$

If the interest rate is the same as the ROA rate, there is no financial leverage gain; there is no spread between the two rates. If the spread is negative (unfavorable), then ROE would be lower as compared with the no-debt/all-equity alternative.

A Middle Course: Moderate Financial Leverage

Assume the business uses a 50/50 mix of debt and equity; that is, its *debt to equity ratio* is 1 to 1. Assuming a 10.0 percent annual interest rate, the three profiles of the business are shown in Exhibit 9–5.

EXHIBIT 9–4
If Interest Rate Equals (Pre-Tax) ROA

Assets Investment Profile		Profit Profile	
Operating Assets	$1,400,000	Sales Revenue	$2,000,000
Operating Liabilities	$ (400,000)	•	•
Assets Investment	$1,000,000	•	•
		•	•
Capital Sources Profile		•	•
		Operating Profit	$ 160,000
		Interest Expense	$ (120,000)
Debt (at 16.0%)	$ 750,000	Taxable Income	$ 40,000
Equity	$ 250,000	Income Tax Expense	$ (13,600)
Total Capital	$1,000,000	Net Income	$ 26,400

EXHIBIT 9-5
One-To-One Debt To Equity Capital Mix

Assets Investment Profile		Profit Profile	
Operating Assets	$1,400,000	Sales Revenue	$2,000,000
Operating Liabilities	$ (400,000)	·	·
Assets Investment	$1,000,000	·	·
		·	·
		·	·
Capital Sources Profile		·	·
		Operating Profit	$ 160,000
		Interest Expense	$ (50,000)
Debt (at 10.0%)	$ 500,000	Taxable Income	$ 110,000
Equity	$ 500,000	Income Tax Expense	$ (37,400)
Total Capital	$1,000,000	Net Income	$ 72,600

The company's ROE is as follows:

$72,600 Net Income ÷ $500,000 Equity Capital
= 14.52% ROE

This ROE is more than the no-debt situation (10.56 percent). But 14.52 percent still may not be entirely satisfactory to the equity-capital investors in the business. For many years DuPont's annual ROE objective has been 20.0 percent though this is an ambitious goal. How can CAPCO improve its ROE to 20.0 percent?

IMPROVING ROE: THE DUPONT MODEL

Reference was just made to DuPont's 20.0 percent ROE objective, which leads quite naturally to the often cited "DuPont" model. Actually, there are many variations of this well-known model. My particular preference or adaptation is shown in Exhibit 9-6 (which uses the 50/50 debt and equity mix for CAPCO).

The DuPont model (pathway) directs attention to the key factors that determine ROE and permits quick analysis of changes in the factors. First, let's take a quick walk through the illustration.

EXHIBIT 9-6
DuPont Model (Pathway) To ROE

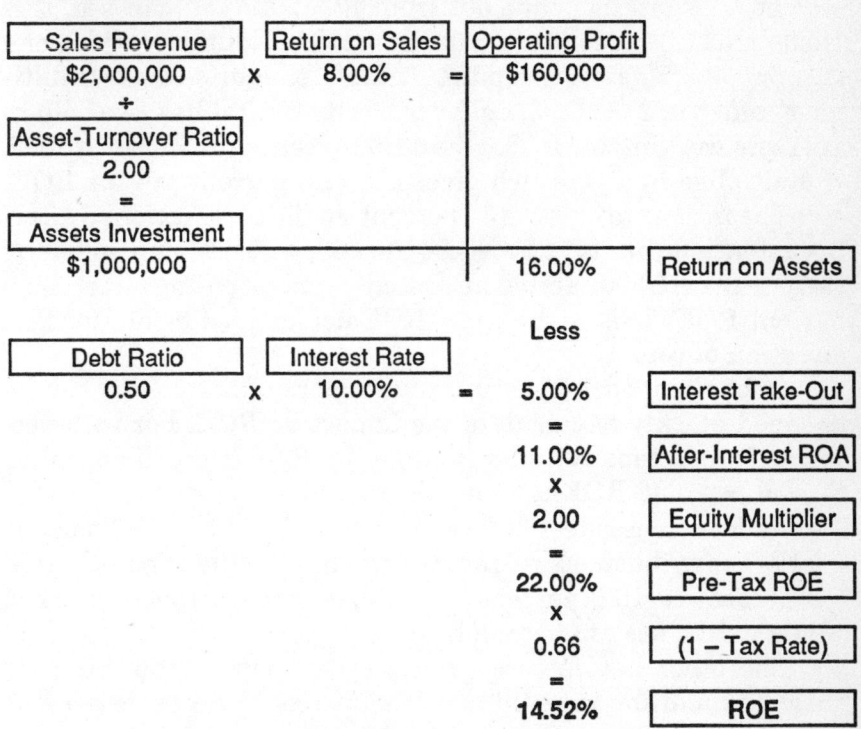

Sales revenue is the starting point, which goes two directions—across to operating profit and down to assets investment. Operating expenses consume 92.0 percent of sales revenue, so the return on sales (ROS) is 8.0 percent. Sales revenue multiplied by ROS yields $160,000 operating profit (before interest and income tax).

In this example the company's annual asset-turnover ratio is 2.0 times, which means sales revenue is twice the company's assets investment. Sales revenue divided by the asset-turnover ratio gives the assets investment of $1,000,000 (operating assets less operating liabilities). Operating profit divided by assets investment gives 16.0 percent ROA (Return on Assets). From this point down, the proportions of debt and equity and the income tax rate determine the final ROE.

In this example debt provides one half or .50 of total capital, which is multiplied times the 10.0 percent interest rate to determine the interest take-out from ROA. As you can see, this yields an 11.0 percent after-interest ROA. Equity provides one half or .50 of the total capital. Therefore, equity has a "multiplier" effect of 2.0.[4] Each dollar of equity capital has two dollars of assets working for it. So, the 11.0 percent after-interest ROA is multiplied by 2.0, which gives the 22.0 percent pre-tax ROE.

The income tax rate is 34 percent, so the corporations's after-tax retention rate is [1.00 − .34], or .66, which is multiplied by the pre-tax ROE to arrive at the after-tax or bottom line 14.52 percent ROE. This is the same ROE determined before for this situation of course.

Once the model is set up, one or more of the factors can be changed quickly to calculate the impact on ROE. For instance, what if the company could improve its ROS (Return on Sales) to 10.0 percent? ROE is shown in Exhibit 9–7.

ROE increases to 19.80 percent, just shy of the 20.0 percent goal of many businesses. Improving the ROS by 2 points from 8.0 percent to 10.0 percent is a 25 percent improvement that would not be easy to accomplish.

The other key factor is the asset-turnover ratio. Suppose CAPCO could improve this ratio 25 percent, the same percent improvement as the change in ROS just examined. Instead of $2.00, there would be $2.50 sales revenue for each $1.00 of assets, or 25 percent more sales revenue per dollar of assets. The asset-turnover ratio would be 2.5 to 1. Thus, CAPCO would need only $800,000 assets investment to support its $2,000,000 sales revenue [$2,000,000 sales revenue ÷ 2.5 = $800,000 assets investment].

CAPCO's operating profit is $160,000. So, its ROA would be 20.0 percent [$160,000 ÷ $800,000 = 20.0 percent]. This is the same ROA that results from improving ROS by 25 percent (see

---

[4] I attribute the term "equity multiplier" to a colleague of mine, Dr. Ron Melicher, Professor of Finance at the University of Colorado at Boulder. I had not heard the term until he had used it several years ago.

EXHIBIT 9–7
ROE If Return On Sales (ROS) Is Improved Two Points

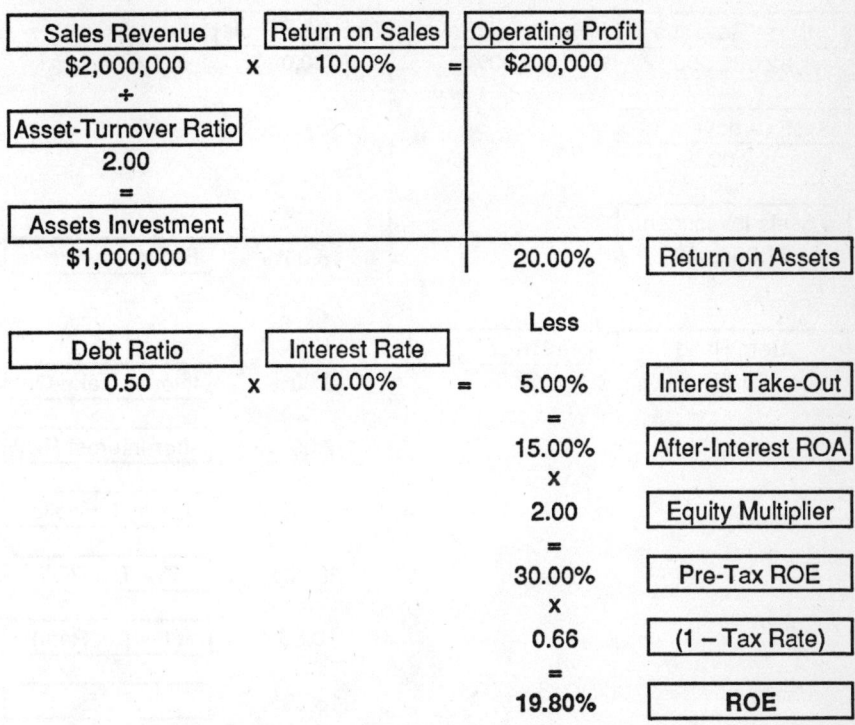

Exhibit 9–7). Therefore, ROE would be the same as before or 19.80 percent. In short, an equal (proportionate change in either the ROS or the asset-turnover ratio) has the same impact on ROE.

Suppose the interest rate had been 12.0 percent and that CAPCO had a three-to-one debt to equity ratio. Otherwise, assume the same factors as before, in particular that ROS is 8.0 percent and the asset-turnover ratio is 2.0. The DuPont model for this scenario is shown in Exhibit 9–8.

As you can see, ROE would be 18.48 percent. You might notice that the equity multiplier is 4.0 because the company has a very high debt-to-equity ratio in this situation. Many other variations on this basic theme can also be played out with the DuPont model.

EXHIBIT 9-8
ROE If Debt to Equity Is 3 To 1 (Interest Rate = 12.0%)

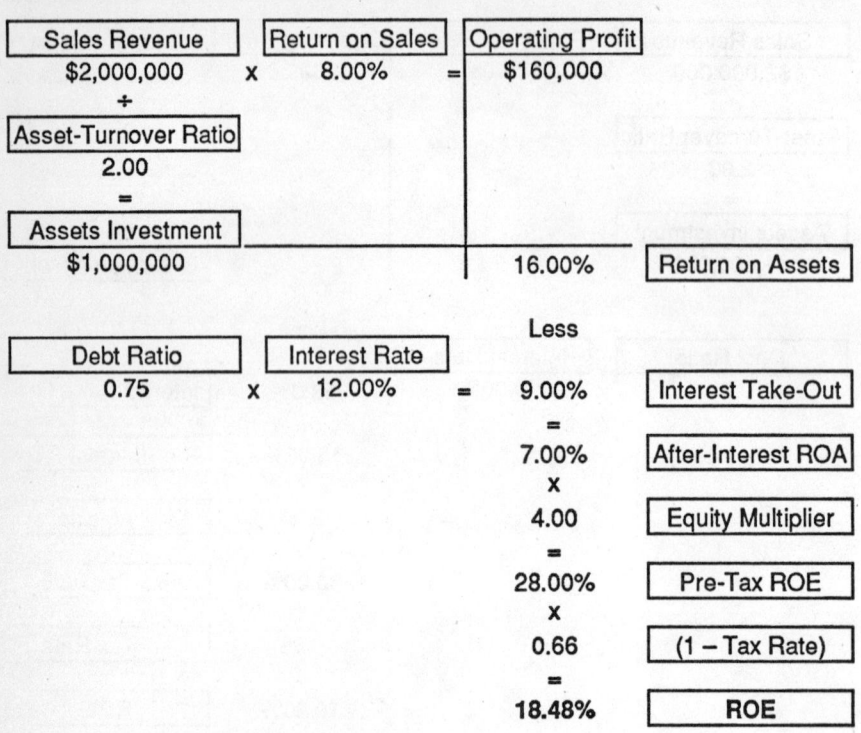

A NOTE ON INCOME TAX

The examples above use the 34 percent maximum marginal income tax rate on corporations under the 1986 Tax Reform Act. However, the business entity, even if it is taxed as an ordinary corporation, may not pay this tax rate on all its taxable income. Lower rates apply on taxable income under $75,000.

Also, a small corporation with less than 35 stockholders may elect to be treated as a "S" corporation, which means its annual taxable income passes through to its stockholders and the corporation itself pays no income tax. Individual stockholders may be in quite different income tax situations. Also, it should be mentioned that business enterprises operating as sole proprietorships and partnerships do not pay federal income tax themselves; they pass through their taxable income to their owner or owners who must include the taxable income on their personal income tax returns.

Corporations may have loss carrybacks and loss carryforwards that reduce or eliminate income tax in any one year. There is also the alternative minimum tax (ATM) to consider, to say nothing of a myriad of other provisions and loopholes in the tax law. CPAs or other tax professionals have to be consulted unless the business has its own tax experts within the organization.

DEBT AND EQUITY VALUES: A FINAL COMMENT

Analyzing financial leverage and ROE, as well as alternative mixes of debt and equity, requires dollar amounts for each. The preceding discussion implicitly assumes *book values* are the correct values for debt and equity. Book values are the account balances reported in the financial statements of the business.

Book values for debt are generally no problem; these are the maturity values of the debt, i.e., the amounts that have to be paid at the maturity date. For financial leverage analysis and for measuring ROE, the maturity values of debt are generally the correct values. And interest rates are based on these values.[5] However, book (maturity) value would not be appropriate if the business is in financial distress, has defaulted on its debt payments, or is in bankruptcy proceedings. Both the business and its lenders have to shift to an entirely different set of projections in these situations.

Book value of equity is usually used for financial leverage analysis. However, keep in mind that book value is *historical* value. The book value of equity is the cumulative sum of paid-in capital amounts (which could go back many years) plus the

---

[5]The one major exception to these comments involves very heavy original issue discount, i.e., when the amount received by the business at the time of borrowing is substantially less than the maturity value of the debt. In these cases, the effective interest rate is materially higher than the interest rate based on maturity value. The effective interest rate should be used; book value should be maturity value less the unamortized discount.

annual additions to Retained Earnings, which is net income less dividends paid each year. If the business has bought back some of its own equity shares, the cost of these "treasury stock" shares is deducted from the sum of paid-in capital and retained earnings; book value of equity is net of the cost of treasury stock.

Corporations do *not* report the effects of financial leverage in their external financial statements. The interested creditor or stockholder has to do this analysis on his or her own. Even in internal management accounting reports, the impact of financial leverage may not be reported nor analyzed. If I were the owner/manager of a business, I would insist that financial leverage analysis be included in my accounting reports. However, in large business organizations many managers do not have any authority or responsibility for how the business is financed (debt versus equity). Financial leverage analysis would not be relevant to them. At the highest level of financial decision making responsibility, however, financial leverage effects should be reported.

ROE is based on book value in external financial reports. That is, net income is divided by book value of equity capital. At this point we should separate between two types of business corporations: publicly owned corporations whose equity shares are actively traded in stock markets, and private or non-public corporations. There are about 10,000 publicly owned corporations in the American economy whose shares are actively traded in organized markets. There are over a million other corporations whose shares are privately held and not traded or traded very seldom.

Private corporations have no ready market value information for their equity capital. (These businesses could make an estimate of the market value or have a formal appraisal done.) By and large they measure ROE on the book value of their equity. But keep in mind that this tends to inflate ROE because the historical book value of equity may be quite low compared with any reasonable estimate of current value.

Publicly owned corporations also report ROE based on the book value of their equity capital. However, stockholders in public corporations have market information. In fact, these stockholders are more interested in two other ratios: the earnings per share (EPS), and the price/earnings (P/E) ratio. EPS is net income divided by the number of common stock shares outstanding. The trend of EPS clearly has more impact on market value of stock shares than ROE. Also, stock investors closely watch the stock's P/E ratio, which is the current market price divided by EPS. In fact, P/E ratios are reported in the *The Wall Street Journal*, whereas, ROE is not. There's no question that ROE (based on book value) takes a back seat to EPS and the P/E ratio for investors in publicly owned corporations.

CHAPTER 10

COST OF CAPITAL AND TIME VALUE OF MONEY

Chapter 9 is the launch pad for this chapter; it explains return on capital and how financial leverage affects return on equity (ROE). In this chapter we assume that the business has settled on its basic debt-to-equity mix of capital (its financial leverage policy) and has established its ROE goals. This premise provides the foundation for determining the *weighted average cost of capital* of the business, which is the *time value of money* benchmark and reference point of business. It's the fundamental rate of return on assets (ROA) that the business should earn to meet its financial objectives.

This chapter examines certain decisions facing business managers in which the time value of money is a key factor in the analysis. The first example is investing in new equipment that will generate future cost savings, a situation in which the cost of capital (time value of money) is certainly a dominant factor. The next example is the lease-versus-buy decision, another case in which the time value of money is the central point of reference. The third main example involves determining the future payments on a note receivable from a customer when the note's interest rate is set lower than the company's cost of capital rate. Many other examples could be examined, but these three cover a broad range of basic issues for business decisions in which the cost of capital and time value of money are the major factors in the analysis.

The approach in the chapter is *non-mathematical;* no formulas are shown. My strong impression is that business managers are not interested in the math or the underlying formulas. They know that necessary computations can be done on business/financial calculators, or in personal computer spreadsheet programs, or by looking up values in compound interest tables.

Managers are interested primarily in the main assumptions and limitations in the decision analysis, which, in my opinion, is exactly the correct management approach. Also, my strong opinion is that managers want to see schedules of future cash flows for these types of decisions, schedules that make very clear the key assumptions and show the breakdown of relevant cash flows period by period. All too often cost of capital and time value of money analytical techniques focus exclusively on one key result, such as the present value or internal rate of return of an investment situation. In my opinion a "single number" approach is not adequate for management decision making, and may even be misleading.

THE WEIGHTED AVERAGE COST OF CAPITAL

As mentioned at the outset, Chapter 9 is the take-off point for this chapter. The basic theme in Chapter 9 is that a business needs to earn enough operating profit on its assets investment so that it can pay the interest on its debt, pay its income tax, and provide enough net income to yield a satisfactory return on its equity capital (ROE). To sum up briefly:

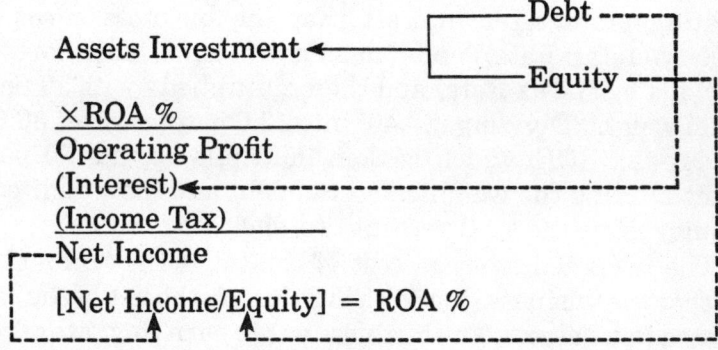

Going in reverse order, we can start with the bottom line ROE rate and work our way back up to the ROA rate necessary to achieve the ROE goal. This "required" ROA rate is called the *weighted average cost of capital*. It is computed from the following factors: the debt-to-equity-capital ratio of the business, the interest rate(s) on its debt, its income-tax rate, and its ROE goal.

For example, assume a 50/50 (1 to 1) debt-to-equity mix, an average 10.0 percent interest rate on debt, a 40 percent (combined federal and state) income-tax rate, and a 18.0 percent after-tax ROE goal. In this situation the weighted average cost of capital is determined as follows:

Weighted Average Cost of Capital

10.0% Interest Rate × 50%	= 5.0%
[18.0% ROE ÷ (1−40% Tax Rate)] = 30.0% × 50%	= 15.0%
Weighted Average Cost of Capital	= 20.0%

To explain: the 10.0 percent interest rate is weighted, or multiplied by 50 percent, which is the ratio of debt-to-total capital. Interest is deductible for income tax, so to pay interest the business has to earn only 10 percent on the one half of its total capital from debt. So, if it earns 10 percent ROA on the one half of its assets supplied by debt, there would be zero taxable income on this part of its operating profit and, thus, no income tax. Equity capital is a quite different matter, however.

The 18.0 percent ROE objective is *after-tax*. A 40 percent tax rate is assumed in this example. Thus, for each $1.00 of operating profit after interest that the business earns, only [$1.00 × (1-Tax Rate)] ends up as net income. Therefore, ROE is divided by (1-Tax Rate) and then multiplied by its 50 percent capital weight. Dividing (1−.40) into 18.0 percent gives 30.0 percent pre-tax ROE, which is then multiplied by its 50 percent weight. Adding the weighted cost of debt and the weighted cost of equity gives the 20.0 percent *average* rate.

The weighted average cost of capital is the "target" ROA rate that the business should earn to justify the use of the capital invested in its assets. The business has to earn this rate of return on its assets investment to "pay for" its capital sources. In this example the business should strive to earn a minimum 20.0 percent ROA; this should serve as its "hurdle rate." If it can do better, fine. It should be reluctant to make asset investments that don't promise at least a 20.0 percent rate of return (operating profit).

Suppose the business has $1,000,000 invested in its assets (operating assets less operating liabilities). And, suppose that it does earn exactly 20.0 percent ROA, or $200,000 operating profit before interest and income tax. Since its ROA equals its weighted average cost of capital, its ROE should be precisely on target. Let's check to make certain that it is:

$200,000 Operating Profit [$1,000,000 Assets × 20.0% RDA]
($50,000) Interest Expense [$500,000 Debt × 10.0%]
($60,000) Income Tax [$150,000 Taxable Income × 40%]
$90,000 Net Income
Check: [$90,000 Net Income/$500,000 Equity] = **18.0% ROE**

As you can see, ROE would be 18.0 percent, which is exactly the ROE goal established by the company.

As mentioned before, the business should use its weighted average cost of capital as the benchmark rate of earnings (profitability) for evaluating investment of capital. This theory is unassailable. However, there are practical problems. Over time the numbers keep changing. The business may shift its ratio of debt-to-equity, interest rates change, tax rates change, and ROE goals may change. Even with these inevitable changes, the weighted average cost of capital may stay within a fairly narrow range.

Looking at the business as a whole—which means looking at the total set of operating assets (less operating liabilities) necessary to carry on its profit making activities—the weighted average cost of capital is the most appropriate time value of money rate for setting operating profit goals. This global or macro view of the business takes into account that its capital sources are a mix of debt and equity, each having different cost of capital rates and each being taxed differently. The weighted average cost of capital rate should be the time value of money test "imposed" on all investments.

DETERMINING THE FUTURE RETURNS NEEDED FROM AN ASSET INVESTMENT

Suppose a retailer is considering purchasing new state-of-the-art, point-of-sale electronic cash registers that read bar-coded information on most of the products the business sells. The business would avoid the labor cost of marking sales prices and sales price changes on its products. And the new registers would also provide better control over the prices charged its customers. (Cashiers sometimes punch in incorrect prices, either by error or intentionally as a "favor" to their friends.)

The future returns on the investment are the labor cost savings; the company's annual cash outlays for labor would decrease if the new cash registers were bought. (The improvements in control provided by the new cash registers is more difficult to quantify.) The cost of the cash registers is $250,000. The retailer decides to adopt a five-year planning horizon for this asset investment. The business thus limits the cost savings to five years, even though there may be benefits beyond this time. However, labor wage rates and other factors are difficult to project beyond a five-year period.

The president of the company asks you to determine how much the labor cost savings would have to be each year, assuming that the savings would be equal every year, to justify the purchase of the new cash registers. The company's weighted average cost of capital is the same as before, or 20.0 percent per year based on its debt-to-capital mix, interest rate, income tax rate, and ROE objective.

There are two main demands on the future cash returns (cost savings): (1) the business must recover the total capital invested in the new assets ($250,000); and (2) the business must earn 20.0 percent ROA each year on the capital balance at the start of the year. Keep in mind that the business does not have $250,000 invested for five years. By imposing a five-year time horizon the business is, in essence, assuming that the new assets will have a five-year useful economic life. The next five years of cost savings have to return the $250,000 capital invested in the assets, plus provide enough to earn 20.0 percent ROA each year on the unrecovered capital balance at the start of the year. That is, each year's cost savings (cash flow) has to provide operating profit (ROA) and capital recovery. The amount of capital recovery at the end of one year reduces the capital balance in the following year. The capital investment decreases year to year; at the end of the last year all the initial capital has been recovered.

Table 10-1 shows the annual labor cost savings amount (cash flow return) that would satisfy the two basic requirements.

Annual labor-cost savings of $83,595 for five years would earn 20.0 percent on the capital investment each year and recover the $250,000 capital invested in the new assets. To explain, consider the second year. At the end of the first year $33,595 capital is recovered; this is the total return (labor cost savings) less the $50,000, or 20.0 percent ROA on the capital investment at the start of the year. Capital recovery reduces the capital investment balance. At the start of the second year, therefore, the unrecovered capital investment is $216,405; 20.0 percent on this balance is $43,281, which is the required ROA amount for the second year. Every year follows this pattern.

The annual cost savings amount can be found with a business/finance calculator (the precise annual return is $83,594.93). However, solving for the amount is not nearly so important as understanding the basic approach and limitations of the method of analysis. As already mentioned, there would be other savings from the better control provided by the new registers that are difficult to estimate. The five-year period is arbitrary; the labor cost savings may continue beyond this time. Or, perhaps the

TABLE 10-1
Annual Labor Cost Savings Needed On Asset Investment

Year	Capital Investment at Start of Year	Capital Recovery	ROA at 20.00%	Labor Cost Savings
1	$250,000	$ 33,595	$50,000	$83,595
2	$216,405	$ 40,314	$43,281	$83,595
3	$176,091	$ 48,377	$35,218	$83,595
4	$127,714	$ 58,052	$25,543	$83,595
5	$ 69,662	$ 69,662	$13,932	$83,595
Total		$250,000		

business will not be able to reduce its labor force as quickly as implied in the analysis. The new registers may provide better inventory control information as well, leading to other cost savings. The company's weighted average cost of capital rate may change during the five years. And so on. These are some of the relevant issues the manager should also consider in the analysis.

The manager should use the type of cash flow schedule shown here as one important source of information in making the decision, but not the only one. The annual labor cost savings amount determined in the schedule does not necessarily settle the decision one way or the other. If the company's employees are unionized, the more immediate problem may be to get the union to agree to installing the registers and working out the concessions for the union's agreement. It is obvious unions understand that automation eliminates jobs.

Nevertheless, such a cash flow schedule is an indispensable point of reference. The manager should ask whether the business could realistically expect to achieve the annual labor cost savings shown in the schedule. In fact, assume you have made a careful study and have estimated that the annual labor cost savings would be as follows: $65,000, $82,500, $95,000, $102,500, and $110,000. The annual returns increase year to year because the business is expecting sales growth and labor-wage rates are also expected to rise. Would the business at least earn its cost of capital based on this forecast of annual returns?

A good first step is to prepare the same sort of cash flow schedule just shown, using the 20.0 percent cost of capital rate, and see what happens (see Table 10-2). There's an error. The total capital recovered is too high; $275,064 is recovered compared with the $250,000 initial capital invested. This means the ROA earned on the investment must be higher than the 20.0 percent rate used in the schedule; excess capital recovery is really additional earnings on the investment.

The next step is to change the ROA rate until exactly $250,000 total capital is recovered (see Table 10-3). If the ROA rate is set exactly at 21.66 percent, the total capital recovery is exactly $250,000, which it should be. This rate is called the *internal rate of return*. It's the rate of earnings on the capital investment, given the forecast of future returns on the investment. It can be solved for with a business/financial calculator or

TABLE 10-2
Annual Labor Cost Savings On Asset Investment

Year	Capital Investment at Start of Year	Capital Recovery	ROA at 20.00%	Labor Cost Savings
1	$250,000	$ 15,000	$50,000	$ 65,000
2	$235,000	$ 35,500	$47,000	$ 82,500
3	$199,500	$ 55,100	$39,900	$ 95,000
4	$144,400	$ 73,620	$28,880	$102,500
5	$ 70,780	$ 95,844	$14,156	$110,000
Total		$275,064		

TABLE 10-3
Annual Labor Cost Savings On Asset Investment

Year	Capital Investment at Start of Year	Capital Recovery	ROA at 21.66%	Labor Cost Savings
1	$250,000	$ 10,857	$54,143	$ 65,000
2	$239,143	$ 30,708	$51,792	$ 82,500
3	$208,434	$ 49,859	$45,141	$ 95,000
4	$158,575	$ 68,157	$34,343	$102,500
5	$ 90,418	$ 90,418	$19,582	$110,000
Total		$250,000		

in a computer-spreadsheet program. But, as said before, the manager should be more concerned with the interpretation of the cash flow schedule and the assumptions and limitations of the analysis.

One thing may have caught your attention in the cash flow schedules. Either of the two situations can be used to make this point. Let's use the first one in which the annual labor cost savings are $83,595. Notice the capital recovery amounts each year in Table 10-1, which are as follows: $33,595, $40,314, $48,377, $58,052, and $69,662. Unfortunately, this capital recovery schedule is somewhat, though not entirely, inconsistent with one assumption in the computation of the weighted average cost of capital rate.

The income tax factor in the weighted average cost of capital computation makes certain assumptions about taxable income each year. Let's look at the first year to follow through on this point. The total return (cost savings) before interest and income tax is $83,595. The capital investment at the start of the year is $250,000, one half from debt and one half from equity capital. Interest for the year is $12,500 [$125,000 debt × 10.0% interest rate = $12,500]. Taxable income, income tax, and net income is as follows:

Breakout of Cost Savings for First Year—To Show Income Tax

Cost Savings	$83,595
Interest Expense (see above)	(12,500)
Depreciation (Equal to Capital Recovery)	33,595
Taxable Income	$37,500
Income Tax (40% × Taxable Income)	(15,000)
Net Income	$22,500

Check:

$22,500 Net Income/$125,000 Equity Capital = 18.0% ROE

Everything looks correct; net income yields 18.0 percent ROE, which is exactly the rate built into the computation of the weighted average cost of capital rate earlier in the chapter.

But notice that the depreciation deduction equals the capital recovery for the year; this is the implicit assumption built into the cost of capital computation that causes the problem here. This is seldom true, and certainly not true in this case. Assume the business uses the straight-line depreciation method with a zero salvage value; its annual depreciation deductions for income tax would be $50,000 ($250,000 cost ÷ 5 years). Compared with the straight-line depreciation amounts, the capital recovery amounts are lower in the first three years and higher in the last two years.

Theoretically, such timing differences between income tax depreciation and capital recovery amounts should be taken into account in the analysis. Investment analysis is built on many estimates and arbitrary assumptions. It's not really all that precise to begin with, and not all factors are included in the numbers. Adding one more layer of numbers (for the timing differences between tax depreciation and capital recovery) may or may not contribute that much additional value to the decision-making process. The manager will have to decide this question.

LEASE OR BUY?

Suppose a business needs to replace certain operating assets; the cost of the new assets is just over a million dollars or $1,015,821, to be precise. The vendor offers an alternative: The business could sign a five-year lease/purchase contract on the assets. The business would make quarterly lease payments of $80,000 at the end of every three months and have the option at the end of the lease to purchase the assets at the bargain price of $50,000. (The assets probably would have a higher value then).

The president of the business puts you in charge of this decision: Should you buy or lease? The business could raise the million dollars capital from its debt and equity sources. Or, for that matter, it may already have the million dollars on hand. If the business were in desperate straits and couldn't raise the million dollars, the lease may be the only alternative. But even in this case, you should do some basic analysis on the lease.

The lease would require 20 payments of $80,000 plus a final payment of $50,000 to purchase the assets, which adds up to total cash outlays of $1,650,000 compared with the purchase cost of just over $1,000,000. This comparison, however, doesn't consider the time value of money. You can't compare a one million dollar cash outlay today with a five-year series of quarterly cash outlays. The time value of money must be brought into the analysis.

Assume the company's weighted average cost of capital is 20.0 percent, the same as computed earlier. There are three basic possibilities relative to the cost of capital rate: (1) the company's actual ROA is very close to its cost of capital; (2) the business is actually earning an ROA higher than its cost of capital; or, (3) the business is falling below its ROA objective. Call these the higher, equal, and lower cases; assume the ROAs for the three are 25.0 percent, 20.0 percent, and 15.0 percent respectively.

A lease is one way that a business can finance the acquisition of assets instead of raising capital from its normal debt and equity sources. Lease payments include (in part) a series of "capital paybacks," or returns of capital to the lessor who is the source of capital for the assets. Clearly the lessor charges a cost of capital rate, which is built into the lease payments. You should determine this rate, and compare it with your cost of capital rate and your actual ROA rate.

Starting with the $1,015,821 purchase cost of the assets and using the $80,000 quarterly lease payments, Table 10-4 shows the ROA rate earned by the lessor. Notice that the final (20th) lease payment also includes the $50,000 purchase payment at the end of the lease. The basic format of the schedule is the same as before: The future cash flows have to recover the capital invested in the assets as well as provide earnings on the unrecovered capital each period. Earnings are measured by the ROA rate; finding this rate is the main purpose of the analysis.

TABLE 10–4
Determining The ROA Earned By Lessor

Payment Number	Investment Balance	Capital Recovered	Earnings at 5.0% Per Period	Lease Payment
1	$1,015,821	$ 29,209	$ 50,791	$ 80,000
2	$ 986,612	$ 30,669	$ 49,331	$ 80,000
3	$ 955,943	$ 32,203	$ 47,797	$ 80,000
4	$ 923,740	$ 33,813	$ 46,187	$ 80,000
5	$ 889,927	$ 35,504	$ 44,496	$ 80,000
6	$ 854,423	$ 37,279	$ 42,721	$ 80,000
7	$ 817,145	$ 39,143	$ 40,857	$ 80,000
8	$ 778,002	$ 41,100	$ 38,900	$ 80,000
9	$ 736,902	$ 43,155	$ 36,845	$ 80,000
10	$ 693,747	$ 45,313	$ 34,687	$ 80,000
11	$ 648,434	$ 47,578	$ 32,422	$ 80,000
12	$ 600,856	$ 49,957	$ 30,043	$ 80,000
13	$ 550,899	$ 52,455	$ 27,545	$ 80,000
14	$ 498,444	$ 55,078	$ 24,922	$ 80,000
15	$ 443,366	$ 57,832	$ 22,168	$ 80,000
16	$ 385,534	$ 60,723	$ 19,277	$ 80,000
17	$ 324,811	$ 63,759	$ 16,241	$ 80,000
18	$ 261,052	$ 66,947	$ 13,053	$ 80,000
19	$ 194,104	$ 70,295	$ 9,705	$ 80,000
20	$ 123,810	$ 123,810	$ 6,190	$ 130,000
Totals		$1,015,821	$634,179	$1,650,000

Notice that the total capital recovered amount at the bottom of this schedule is exactly equal to the initial capital invested ($1,015,821). Therefore the ROA is 5.0 percent per quarter, or 20.0 percent per year. The business, therefore, would be paying the lessor a 20.0 percent cost of capital rate. Determining the lessor's ROA rate provides a very essential piece of information; the business needs to compare the lessor's ROA against its own cost of capital and actual ROA.

You may be curious how the 20.0 percent rate was determined. One way is to use a business/finance calculator. Also, a computer-spreadsheet program can be easily prepared to solve for the 20.0 percent rate; just keep changing the rate until the total capital recovered comes out exactly equal to the initial cost of the assets. The more important point for managers, as stated before, is to understand the basic approach of this analysis rather than to do the calculations. The manager should be able to follow the schedule shown above, and be aware of the assumptions and limitations of the analysis.

In fact, one key assumption should be pointed out here: The assets are assumed to have no terminal value at the end of the lease, which would be true for the lessor, but may not be true for the business (lessee). Projecting asset values five years down the road is tricky, to say the least. However, the manager should make some estimate. Suppose that your best estimate is that the assets will have $200,000 value at the end of the lease. In fact, this is why you would be willing to purchase the assets at the end of the lease for the bargain price of $50,000. This makes the lease more attractive to the business.

Lease-versus-buy decisions are more complicated than the essential features discussed above. There's the matter of who pays for insurance, property taxes (if any), and repair and maintenance costs over the life of the lease. The legal contract may have many other provisions, options, as well as penalty clauses that may or may not come into play. The business may decide two or three years later that it no longer needs the assets, which would require breaking the lease or paying a penalty to exit early.

And, there is accounting factor to consider. This lease would be recorded as a *capital lease,* which means the lease would be recorded as a purchase of assets on the one side of the Balance Sheet and as a long-term debt obligation on the other side. The assets would be depreciated, and lease payments would be separated into principal reduction and interest expense. The manager may prefer to keep the lease "off the books" or off the Balance Sheet. But accountants have drawn up fairly tight rules; only *operating* leases can be kept off the books; these leases cannot run for such a large part of the assets' useful lives. Operating leases are short-term rentals, not long-term leases with purchase options. In short, an operating lease is not an alternative to buying the asset.

Summing up, the business should compare the lessor's ROA included in the lease payments with its own cost of capital benchmark and its actual ROA. The lease is essentially an alternative to using its own capital, so the actual ROA being earned on its assets investment is the main point for comparison. If the business is earning 25.0 percent ROA on all the capital it can raise, then the lease may be attractive as a cheaper source of capital. If the business is earning only 15.0 percent ROA, its first problem is to improve its profit performance, as previous chapters discuss. Taking on a lease with a 20.0 percent cost of capital would only make matters worse, unless this were strictly a stop-gap measure that would lead to improvement in the overall ROA of the business. But how? If the company's actual ROA were close to 20.0 percent, the lease-versus-buy decision boils down to a source of capital question, which gets into the broader field of business finance.

NOTES RECEIVABLE FROM CUSTOMERS

Introduction: Two Alternative Loan–Payment Schedules

Suppose this business sells a very high-priced product. Many of its customers need long-term credit stretching three years or more. The business has just closed a sales contract with one of its best customers for products having a total sales price of $150,000. The customer can make a down payment of $30,000, but needs to arrange a loan for the balance. The customer agrees to sign a three-year interest-bearing note to the business calling for payments at the end of every three months (a total of 12 quarterly payments). The customer has a good credit rating, so the business agrees to accept the note for $120,000.

What rate of interest should the business charge on this note? Assume its weighted average cost of capital rate is the 20.0 percent rate computed above. This rate would look very high to the customer, and might, in fact, discourage the customer from buying the products. Suppose the going interest rate on this type of "paper" is 12.0 percent.

For the moment we'll assume the business agrees to the 12.0 percent annual interest rate. This is the annual percentage rate (APR) which has to adjust to fit the frequency of payment. In this example payments are made quarterly, so the interest rate is 3.0 percent per quarter. The APR is divided by the number of payments per year to get the *effective* interest rate per payment period.

Not one but two note payment schedules are presented here; the two are compared to illustrate several important points. Typically, loan payments are uniform; all payments are the same amount. (A series of equal payments at equal intervals is called an *annuity.*) Instead of equal loan payments, however, the loan payments could be set so that the principal reduction is equal every period. These two alternative loan payment schedules are presented on the next page (See Table 10-5).

The top schedule is the uniform principal reduction case; every loan payment includes $10,000 principal reduction. The loan balance decreases $10,000 each period, so interest decreases $300 each period. Thus, the loan payment decreases $300 each period. Of course, interest is based on the loan balance at the start of each period, which is called the *effective-interest-rate method.* For instance, at the start of the fifth period the loan balance is $80,000, so the interest for this period is $2,400 ($80,000 × 3.0%).[1]

---

[1] Interest based on the initial or original loan balance is called "simple" interest. In this example, the simple interest would be $120,000 × 12.0% = $14,400 per year, times 3 years for total interest of $43,200. Compare this with the total interest amounts shown in the note payment schedules; notice how much difference there is between simple interest and effective interest. Virtually all business finance is based on effective interest, although you can't be too careful and should make certain if there is any doubt.

TABLE 10-5
Two Note Receivable Payment Schedules

Uniform Principal Reduction Amounts
Interest Rate = 12.0% Per Year (3.0% per Quarter)

Payment Number	Loan (Principal) Balance	Principal Reduction	Interest	Loan Payment
1	$120,000	$ 10,000	$ 3,600	$ 13,600
2	$110,000	$ 10,000	$ 3,300	$ 13,300
3	$100,000	$ 10,000	$ 3,000	$ 13,000
4	$ 90,000	$ 10,000	$ 2,700	$ 12,700
5	$ 80,000	$ 10,000	$ 2,400	$ 12,400
6	$ 70,000	$ 10,000	$ 2,100	$ 12,100
7	$ 60,000	$ 10,000	$ 1,800	$ 11,800
8	$ 50,000	$ 10,000	$ 1,500	$ 11,500
9	$ 40,000	$ 10,000	$ 1,200	$ 11,200
10	$ 30,000	$ 10,000	$ 900	$ 10,900
11	$ 20,000	$ 10,000	$ 600	$ 10,600
12	$ 10,000	$ 10,000	$ 300	$ 10,300
Totals		$120,000	$23,400	$143,400

Uniform Loan Payments
Interest Rate = 12.0% Per Year (3.0% per Quarter)

Payment Number	Loan (Principal) Balance	Principal Reduction	Interest	Loan Payment
1	$120,000	$ 8,455	$ 3,600	$ 12,055
2	$111,545	$ 8,709	$ 3,346	$ 12,055
3	$102,835	$ 8,970	$ 3,085	$ 12,055
4	$ 93,865	$ 9,239	$ 2,816	$ 12,055
5	$ 84,626	$ 9,517	$ 2,539	$ 12,055
6	$ 75,109	$ 9,802	$ 2,253	$ 12,055
7	$ 65,307	$ 10,096	$ 1,959	$ 12,055
8	$ 55,210	$ 10,399	$ 1,656	$ 12,055
9	$ 44,811	$ 10,711	$ 1,344	$ 12,055
10	$ 34,100	$ 11,032	$ 1,023	$ 12,055
11	$ 23,068	$ 11,363	$ 692	$ 12,055
12	$ 11,704	$ 11,704	$ 351	$ 12,055
Totals		$120,000	$24,665	$144,665

One advantage of the uniform principal reduction case is that you can easily see how the loan payment amounts are determined. Each payment is the sum of the $10,000 principal reduction plus interest on the loan balance at the start of the period. Schedules should have this "readability" feature for management decision-making analysis. In contrast, the loan payment amount in the second schedule is not as easy to figure out, is it?

In fact, is it the correct amount? Yes, it must be correct because the total principal reduction over the life of the note is exactly $120,000, and your interest is 3.0 percent of the loan balance at the start of each period (quarter).

How would you determine the $12,055 uniform payment amount (or $12,055.45, to be more precise)? Well, an even more basic question is whether the business manager *should* solve for the amount.

A business/finance calculator, e.g., the HP 12C or 17B, can be used to find the amount in a matter of seconds. But is this the function of the business manager? A manager doesn't make money by doing calculations such as this, but rather by making the correct decisions. The manager has to decide whether to extend long-term credit to customers in the first place, decide the interest rate to charge, decide how to price the products in anticipation of the customer's need for long-term credit, and consider alternatives to carrying the paper (holding the note receivable for the life of the loan). Schedules such as the ones shown are available at the push of a button. Making the best choices is not so easy.

Perhaps the business could take the note receivable to its bank and borrow against it. Suppose it borrows $120,000 at 12.0 percent interest per year and makes quarterly payments. In this case, the business is using a "match-up" approach; a specific asset investment is matched up with a specific source of capital. Basically, the business "breaks even" on the note receivable from its customer. The business is mainly a middleman or conduit receiving cash from its customer and immediately paying the cash out to the bank. The business may have better credit standing with the bank than its customer.

Or, the business could originate the loan and immediately sell the note (a negotiable instrument) to a bank or other financial institution that specializes in this type of loan. Car dealers and other businesses do this, and they get a fee for originating the loan. I worked on a Ford dealership audit some years ago. The dealer made more profit from originating car loans than from selling cars. The business has to screen customers and process some paperwork, but the cost of doing this is relatively small.

A business may set up its own finance company subsidiary to make product-purchase loans to its customers. The strategy here is that the loan business is very different from manufacturing and selling products. Also, the capitalization of the finance subsidiary is usually a very different mix of debt and equity as compared with the main business itself. Finance subsidiaries often have a much higher ratio of debt to equity, and may have a lower weighted average cost of capital.

Suppose, however, the business carries the note receivable itself and charges only 12.0 percent annual interest, even though its weighted average cost of capital is 20.0 percent per year. Does this mean a "loss" on the note? Well, this depends. Suppose you're the sales manager and from experience you know that most customers will ask to finance their purchases, and they will expect the going interest rate on the note. How should you deal with this?

One strategy would be to "jack up" the sales price, to provide the extra amount needed to make up for the difference between your cost of capital rate and the note's interest rate. You would hold to this sales price for customers that demand financing, but would be willing to give a discount to those customers willing to pay cash. In fact, assume that the $150,000 sales price given above is the *credit* sales price. That is, it includes an added amount to make up for the difference between the cost of capital rate and the lower interest rate on the note.

Now, assume that a different customer is willing to pay cash for the same products and wants a discount from the credit price. How much discount would you be willing to give?

Discounting the Credit Price to Determine the Cash Price

The situation is this: The credit price is $150,000, based on a down payment of $30,000 and a three-year note receivable for the $120,000 balance. The credit price is based on a 12.0 percent interest rate on the note, which gives quarterly payments of $12,055 (assuming uniform-loan payments). This interest rate is less than the 20.0 percent cost of capital for the business. We need to determine the *cash* price that you would be willing to sell for. The $30,000 down payment is the same for both; the problem is converting the $120,000 loan balance into an equivalent cash amount based on the 20.0 percent time value of money to the business.

Table 10-6 keeps the quarterly loan payments the same, but changes the annual interest rate to 20.0 percent or 5.0 percent per quarter (equal to the weighted average cost of capital).

At the higher interest rate more of each loan payment has to go for interest, which leaves less for principal reduction. Thus, the initial loan balance decreases to $106,850. In short, your cash price should be $136,850 [$30,000 down payment + ($106,850 @ 20.0%)] which is equivalent to the credit price of $150,000 [$30,000 + ($120,000 @ 12.0%)].

You may be asking yourself again how to determine the initial loan balance of $106,850. This requires just a few keystrokes on a business/financial calculator. Key in the loan payment ($12,055), the number of periods (12), and the interest rate

TABLE 10-6
Loan Payment Schedule At 20.0% Interest Rate

Uniform Loan Payments
Interest Rate = 20.0% Per Year (5.0% per Quarter)

Payment Number	Loan (Principal) Balance	Principal Reduction	Interest	Loan Payment
1	$106,850	$ 6,713	$ 5,343	$ 12,055
2	$100,137	$ 7,049	$ 5,007	$ 12,055
3	$ 93,089	$ 7,401	$ 4,654	$ 12,055
4	$ 85,688	$ 7,771	$ 4,284	$ 12,055
5	$ 77,917	$ 8,160	$ 3,896	$ 12,055
6	$ 69,757	$ 8,568	$ 3,488	$ 12,055
7	$ 61,189	$ 8,996	$ 3,059	$ 12,055
8	$ 52,194	$ 9,446	$ 2,610	$ 12,055
9	$ 42,748	$ 9,918	$ 2,137	$ 12,055
10	$ 32,830	$ 10,414	$ 1,641	$ 12,055
11	$ 22,416	$ 10,935	$ 1,121	$ 12,055
12	$ 11,481	$ 11,481	$ 574	$ 12,055
Totals		$106,850	$37,815	$144,665

(20.0%), and then hit the key for the *present value* amount. Actually, I already had entered the example in a computer spreadsheet, so I just changed the interest rate and printed out the new schedule. But, to repeat an earlier point, managers don't make money by knowing how to work a calculator or how to use a spreadsheet program. These are helpful tools of the trade, but the manager's function goes far beyond knowing how to use these tools.

PART 3

A FINAL WORD

CHAPTER 11

MANAGEMENT CONTROL

WHAT'S AHEAD

To this point the book has concentrated on profit and financial analysis for decision making. This last chapter of the book shifts attention to *management control*. Decision making lays down a plan of action for accomplishing objectives. Reaching the objectives requires management control.

In the broadest sense management control refers to everything managers do in moving the business towards its objectives. Above all else, management control is goal oriented. Management control is both preventive and positive in nature. Managers have to prevent, or at least minimize, wrong things from happening, and they have to make certain that right things are happening and happening on time.

The preventive side of management control begins with *accounting controls*. These procedures are instituted to minimize (ideally, to eliminate) errors in capturing, processing, storing, and retrieving the large amount of detailed financial information needed to run a business. Keep in mind that the accounting system is the source of information

- For operating day to day (paying bills on time, meeting the payroll, sending reminders to past due receivables, etc.),
- For management decision making,
- For preparing management control reports,
- For preparing external financial statements, and
- For preparing tax returns.

The reliability of the accounting system depends in great measure on the controls built into the system and how well the controls are working.

Accounting controls also include safeguards and procedures designed to protect against theft and fraud by employees, suppliers, customers, and, yes, even by managers themselves. Unfortunately, I've found that my father-in-law was correct. He told me many years ago that based on his business experience, "There's a little bit of larceny in everyone's heart." In fact, I've discovered there's a lot of larceny in the hearts of a few.

It's an unpleasant fact of business life that, given the opportunity, some customers will shoplift, some vendors will overcharge or short-count on deliveries, some employees will embezzle, and some managers will commit fraud against the business or take personal advantage of their positions of authority in the business. Controls are designed to minimize such opportunities, and to make it more difficult for anyone to get away with it. However, no control is foolproof. When preventive controls are defeated, which should not be very often, the business needs to have procedures in place to detect the dishonesty quickly.

Managers don't rely just on accounting controls. They depend on a very broad range of information sources and they use many tactics for accomplishing their goals. Managers monitor employee absenteeism, production schedules, quality-control-inspection results, and so on. Job applicants are carefully screened; for instance, lie-detector tests may be used as part of the hiring process. Managers listen to customers' complaints, shop the competition, and may even decide that some industrial intelligence and espionage is necessary. This chapter can't cover the whole waterfront; this chapter focuses on accounting controls and the financial information needed for management control.

Management control requires feedback information; managers must keep close watch on actual progress towards goals, and know when and where things start to go wrong. Control reports should closely follow the decision-making thinking of the managers. Control reports should show clearly how decisions are actually working out over time, in particular, how much better or worse than planned. In short, decision making sets the stage for the type of control information needed by managers.

Budgeting is the epitome of integrating decision making and control. Decisions are made explicit in a budget, which is the concrete plan of action for achieving the profit and financial objectives of the business according to a timetable. Actual results are evaluated against the budget period by period, line by line, and item by item. Variances have to be explained; variances serve as the catalyst for taking corrective action where needed, or for revising the plan.

No budgeting doesn't mean lack of control. Budgeting is helpful but not essential for management control. There are many businesses that use little or no budgeting, yet they make a good profit and remain solvent and financially healthy. They depend on control reports to track their actual profit performance and financial position. But there is no budget against which to compare actual results.

The previous (decision-making) chapters of the book are reexamined from the management control point of view. The main theme is that the design of control reports should be guided by the decision-making thinking of managers. Control reports should resonate on the decisions that are guiding the basic course of the business. The structure and content of control reports should, therefore, conform closely with the decision-making analyses of managers.

The income statement reported externally to creditors and investors serves as the model for the typical accounting profit control report to managers. Most internal profit reports resemble the external income statement, with the main difference being that the internal report contains a lot more detail. This is a serious problem. The structure of the external income statement is a very poor framework for designing management profit control reports; this format doesn't conform with the decision making of managers. Managers make decisions one way, and then get reports that present profit performance another way. Guidelines are offered to correct this basic impediment to effective management control.

ACCOUNTING CONTROLS

Quite naturally CPA auditors are very concerned with accounting controls. Based on their audit findings, they "certify" or express an opinion on the financial statements of a business. In essence, the CPA auditor assures creditors and investors that they can rely on the financial statements issued by the business, that proper accounting methods and disclosure standards have been followed in preparing the financial report. If the financial statements are later discovered to have been misleading or incomplete, the auditors are liable to those creditors and investors who suffered losses.

Financial statements depend on the completeness, timeliness, and accuracy of the accounting records from which the statements are prepared. Accounting controls must be established and enforced to prevent errors and to deter fraud. Naturally managers should be equally concerned with the reliability of their accounting systems and with the prevention of dishonesty.

In rough terms, accounting controls have two broad purposes: (1) to make the accounting system reliable and as error-free as possible; and, (2) to protect against dishonesty. Recently the national organization of CPAs, the American Institute of Certified Public Accountants, released an important authoritative pronouncement dealing with accounting controls. It's an excellent summary and reflects the long experience of CPAs in auditing a very wide range of businesses. We won't look at the auditing aspects; our concern is with those parts most relevant to management control.

One word of explanation: The pronouncement uses the umbrella term "internal control structure," which refers to the environment of control as well as the accounting system and control procedures built into the system. Our interest is mainly with accounting controls.

From the AICPA's Recent Official Statement Regarding Accounting Controls:[1] [Paragraph numbers are from the official statement; emphases supplied are not in the original.]

> 9. The *control environment* represents the collective effect of various factors on establishing, enhancing, or mitigating

---

[1] Auditing Standards Board, "Consideration of the Internal Control Structure in a Financial Statement Audit," *Statement on Auditing Standards 55* (April 1988) (N.Y.: Am. Institute of Certified Public Accountants, Inc., 1988), pp. 5–8.

the effectiveness of specific policies and procedures. Such factors include the following:

- Management's *philosophy* and *operating style*
- The entity's *organizational structure*
- The functioning of the board of directors and its committees, particularly the *audit committee*
- Methods of assigning *authority and responsibility*
- Management's control methods for monitoring and following up on performance, including *internal auditing*
- Personnel policies and practices
- Various *external influences* that affect an entity's operations and practices, such as examinations by bank regulatory agencies.

The control environment reflects the overall attitude, awareness, and actions of the board of directors, management, owners, and others concerning the importance of control and its emphasis in the entity. . . .

10. The *accounting system* consists of the methods and records established to identify, assemble, analyze, classify, record, and report an entity's transactions and to maintain accountability for the related assets and liabilities. An effective accounting system gives appropriate consideration to establishing methods and records that will—

- Identify and record *all valid transactions*
- Describe on a *timely basis* the transactions in *sufficient detail* to permit proper classification of transactions for financial reporting
- Measure the value of transactions in a manner that permits recording their *proper monetary value* in the financial statements
- Determine the *time period* in which transactions occurred to permit recording of transactions in the proper accounting period
- Present properly the transactions and related *disclosures* in the financial statements. . . .

11. *Control procedures* are those policies and procedures in addition to the control environment and accounting systems that management has established to provide rea-

sonable assurance that specific entity objectives will be achieved. Control procedures have various objectives and are applied at various organization and data processing levels. They may also be integrated into specific components of the control environment and the accounting system. Generally, they may be categorized as procedures that pertain to

- Proper *authorization* of transactions and activities
- *Segregation of duties* that reduce the opportunities to allow any person to be in a position to both perpetrate and conceal errors or irregularities in the normal course of his duties--assigning *different people* the responsibilities of *authorizing* transactions, *recording* transactions, and *maintaining custody* of assets
- Design and use of adequate *documents and records* to help ensure the proper recording of transactions and events, such as monitoring the use of prenumbered shipping documents
- Adequate safeguards over *access to and use of assets* and records, such as secured facilities and authorization to access to computer programs and data files
- *Independent checks* on performance and proper valuation of recorded amounts, such as clerical checks, reconciliations, comparison of assets with recorded accountability, computer-programmed controls, management review of reports that summarize the detail of account balances (for example, an aged trial balance of accounts receivable), and user review of computer-generated reports. . . .

(12.) a formal written *code of conduct* or an *organizational structure* that provides for formal delegation of authority may be significant to the control environment of a large entity. However, a *small entity* with effective owner-manager involvement may not need a formal code or organizational structure. Similarly, a small entity with effective owner-manager involvement may not need extensive accounting procedures, sophisticated accounting records, or formal control procedures, such as a formal credit policy, information security policy, or competitive bidding procedures. . . .

(14.) Although the *cost-benefit relationship* is a primary criterion that should be considered in designing an internal control structure, the precise measurement of costs and benefits usually is not possible. Accordingly, management makes both quantitative and qualitative estimates and judgments in evaluating the cost-benefit relationship.

(15.) The potential effectiveness of an entity's internal control structure is subject to *inherent limitations*. Mistakes in the application of policies and procedures may arise from such causes as misunderstanding of instructions, mistakes in judgment, and personal carelessness, distraction, or fatigue. Furthermore, the policies and procedures that require segregation of duties can be circumvented by collusion among persons both within and outside the entity and by management override of certain policies or procedures. . . .

These comments provide an excellent checklist of the types of accounting controls that a business should establish, and enforce!

BUDGETING IN BRIEF

Nature of Budgeting

As mentioned before, decisions lay down a plan of action or strategy for achieving profit and financial objectives. Decisions can be compared to the blueprint of a building. Control is carried out in the context of the decision "blueprint." Decisions are the reference point and the framework for management control. Budgeting is the "perfect example" of integrating decision making with management control.

The larger the organization, the more likely you'll find a formal and comprehensive financial budgeting process in place. Strategic planning is put in the form of a detailed overall budget. The budget is the primary means of communication and authorization down the line in the organization. The budget provides the benchmarks for evaluating performance of managers at all levels. Actual is compared against budget; variances are highlighted. Significant variances are investigated and reported up the line. Managers are rewarded for meeting the budget and are held accountable for unfavorable variances.

Many books have been written on budgeting. There are many advantages and uses of budgeting. But budgeting is costly, and may lead to a lot of "game playing" and dysfunctional behavior. Some reasons for budgeting are not applicable to smaller businesses, in particular, the communication and coordination purposes that are so important in larger organizations where top management is distant from day-to-day operations. The many aspects and procedures of budgeting for larger organizations are not discussed here. Rather, a few fundamentals which apply to all businesses are discussed.

Profit Budgeting

Budgeting depends very much on the ability of managers to forecast changes in the key factors that drive profit. To illustrate this point, let's return to the company example introduced in Chapter 3. Its Profit Profile for the year just ended is reproduced in Table 11-1.

Last year's results provide the point of departure for budgeting next year's operating profit. Assume the basic goal is to increase operating profit to $175,000 next year. The manager makes the following forecasts: Product cost will increase 10 per-

TABLE 11-1
Actual Results For Last Year

Annual Sales Volume	1,000 units	
Annual Break-even Volume	680 units	
Annual Capacity Volume	1,250 units	
	Per Unit	Total
Sales Revenue	$ 2,000	$ 2,000,000
Product Cost	$(1,200)	$(1,200,000)
Variable Expenses	$ (300)	$ (300,000)
Profit Margin	$ 500	$ 500,000
Fixed Expenses		$ (340,000)
Operating Profit		$ 160,000

cent, variable expenses will increase 8 percent, and, fixed expenses will decrease 5 percent (due to some early retirements and cost saving moves).

Without any increases in sales price or sales volume, operating profit would drop to $33,000 as the result of these changes. (You might want to check this, especially if you have already set up a spreadsheet for this example.) Obviously, either sales price or sales volume, or some combination of both will have to be improved to achieve the operating profit goal of $175,000 next year. The manager estimates that the company would not meet any price resistance up to $2,100, so this sales price is "plugged into" the profit budget profile. At this sales price a sales volume will have to be 1,093 units next year.

In short, a sales volume increase of just over 9 percent would be needed, which the manager thinks is possible. The manager decides to "go with" this set of forecasts and goals; this is the budget plan. The operating profit budget for next year is presented in Table 11–2.

This may or not be a good budget, i.e., a good strategy or good decision plan. One aspect I certainly don't like is the $44 decrease in the profit margin per unit. Reaching the operating profit goal depends on increasing sales volume instead of passing on the full amount of cost increases to the sales price, which

TABLE 11–2
Operating Profit Budget For Next Year

	Last Year (Actual)		Next Year (Budget)		Differences	
Annual Sales Volume	1,000 units		1,093 units		93 units	
Annual Break-even Volume	680 units		708 units		28 units	
Annual Capacity Volume	1,250 units		1,250 units		no change	
	Per Unit	Total	Per Unit	Total	Per Unit	Total
Sales Revenue	$ 2,000	$ 2,000,000	$ 2,100	$ 2,295,300	$ 100	$ 295,300
Product Cost	$(1,200)	$(1,200,000)	$(1,320)	$(1,442,760)	$(120)	$(242,760)
Variable Expenses	$ (300)	$ (300,000)	$ (324)	$ (354,132)	$ (24)	$ (54,132)
Profit Margin	$ 500	$ 500,000	$ 456	$ 498,408	$ (44)	$ (1,592)
Fixed Expenses		$ (340,000)		$ (323,000)		$ 17,000
Operating Profit		$ 160,000		$ 175,408		$ 15,408

would preserve the profit margin per unit. Alternatively, you can argue that the sales volume growth is needed just to keep total profit margin about even with last year, and that the reduction of fixed expenses provides the increase in operating profit.

Is this relatively "simple" profit plan really a budget? Well, there is a plan of action based on forecast changes in each key operating profit factor, and there is an operating profit goal. However, there's no budgeted balance sheet at the end of the year and no cash flow budget for next year. Operating profit has been budgeted; but interest expense and income tax have not been budgeted, so the budget does not carry down all the way to the bottom line.

A complete budget or financial plan requires a budgeted year-end balance sheet and a cash flow budget for the coming year. The lessons of Chapter 7 (assets and liabilities) and Chapter 8 (cash flow) provide the essential guidelines for budgeting the ending balance sheet and cash flows for the year. If you refer to these two chapters, you'll see how the budgeting or planning process would be more detailed.

A total financial plan, that is, a profit budget that is tied in with the budgeted ending balance sheet and cash flow budget for the year, is a very convincing package when applying for a loan or renewing existing lines of credit. It shows that the total financial plan has been thought out. The manager may prefer to leave the details to the accountant, but the manager will have to supply all the essential forecasts and assumptions on which the financial budget plan is based.

Budgeting and Controlling Expenses

Many would point out that the expense lines in the operating profit budget shown above are not detailed enough for control purposes. The profit budget is adequate for setting sales prices and sales volume targets. But more detail is needed for controlling expenses. This brings up one key difference between decision making and control.

Decision making has to condense information into a relatively few key factors. Decisions deal with summary level or aggregate data. Decisions cannot deal with the thousand-and-one details that are bound to occur after the plan of action is set into motion. Indeed, it's not possible to anticipate every conceivable contingency. Something new always comes up to surprise you.

In contrast, control must also deal with detail, detail, and more detail. Each key decision factor is the aggregate sum of many specific items making up the factor. Notice that the variable expense factor in the above profit budget is $324.00 per unit. This total amount consists of many different items, perhaps over one-hundred.

Day to day and month to month the manager has to pay attention to an avalanche of details. Keeping all the details in perspective is a challenge, to say the least. Control reports should not let the details take over, causing the manager to lose sight of the overall progress towards the profit goal. The whole point of budgeting, one easy to lose sight of, is to achieve your profit and other financial objectives. Budgeting is not an end in itself.

Detailed expense and cost reporting is required, especially so that the manager can keep close watch on the *total* effect on the key expense and cost factors' forecast in the profit budget. But how frequently should these control reports be prepared and in how much detail? Daily, weekly, monthly, quarterly? Every item over $100, $1,000, $10,000? There are no easy answers. Often managers ask for reams of detailed expense and cost reports, but they may not necessarily read all the detail. Generally speaking, the manager has to rely on the accountant to strike a practical balance between "too much/too frequent" versus "too little/too late" in reporting expenses and costs.

GUIDELINES FOR MANAGEMENT CONTROL REPORTS

The Need For Comparative Reports

More than anything else, management control is directed towards achieving profit goals and meeting the other financial objectives of the business.[2] Goals and objectives are never established in a vacuum. Prior-period performance is the point of departure for developing budgets, except for a start-up business of course. If the business does not use a formal budgeting process, profit and other financial goals are set relative to last year.

In short, *comparative* reports are essential for management control. Actual performance this year is compared against last period, or against the budget for this year. The same idea applies to manufacturers who set standards for product costs. Standards are based on forecast changes and the improvements needed over last period. Actual production costs are compared against standards.

As mentioned before, one of the most basic functions of the manager is to anticipate changes and to make the changes necessary to maintain or improve the profit performance and financial position of the business. Comparative control reports, with their emphasis on changes between periods or variances between budget and actual, are indispensable for management control. In many respects, a master plan (whether or not formalized in a budget) is a "plan of changes." Control reports should, therefore, focus on whether or not the changes are being made according to plan.

For example, consider again the operating profit budget developed earlier in the chapter (see Table 11–2). The manager must closely watch each of the changes. Is the budgeted $2,100 sales price actually holding? Or, is the company having to give discounts or make other price concessions? Is the product actually being purchased (or manufactured) at the budgeted $1,320 per unit, or is the actual cost higher or lower than budgeted? And so on down the line for each key profit factor.

To illustrate these points, assume that the management control report for the year is as shown in Table 11–3. The variances column would attract the most management control attention.

---

[2]I would be remiss here not to mention that some businesses do little or no financial or profit planning. It appears that they decide what to do as they go along. Their objectives are very ill-defined, such as "doing better than last year." Their profit goals may be a little more definite than their financial condition (balance sheet) and cash flow goals. But even their profit goals are very general and vague.

TABLE 11-3
Management Control Report For Year

	Budget		Actual		Variances (Unfavorable)	
Annual Sales Volume	1,093 units		1,105 units		12 units	
Annual Break-even Volume	708 units		739 units		31 units	
Annual Capacity Volume	1,250 units		1,250 units		no change	
	Per Unit	Total	Per Unit	Total	Per Unit	Total
Sales Revenue	$ 2,100	$ 2,295,300	$ 2,050	$ 2,265,250	$(50)	$(30,050)
Product Cost	$(1,320)	$(1,442,760)	$(1,285)	$(1,419,925)	$ 35	$ 22,835
Variable Expenses	$ (324)	$ (354,132)	$ (328)	$ (362,440)	$ (4)	$ (8,308)
Profit Margin	$ 456	$ 498,408	$ 437	$ 482,885	$(19)	$(15,523)
Fixed Expenses		$ (323,000)		$ (323,000)		$ 0
Operating Profit		$ 175,408		$ 159,885		$(15,523)

As you can see, sales volume was slightly over budget, but sales price was under, while variable expenses were over budget. The company fell short of its budgeted operating profit goal by more than $15,000.

One key question concerns how often to prepare control reports. Clearly the manager should not wait until the end of the year, although the end-of-the-year review (such as that just shown) is a good idea. For one thing, it's the platform for developing next year's budget. Daily or weekly control reports are not practical for most businesses, although some companies monitor daily sales volume and other vital operating statistics, such as airlines and banks.

Monthly or quarterly control reports are the most common. This means the budget has to be broken down into monthly or quarterly "slices." In particular, sales volume quotas must be forecast for each interim period, and fixed expenses have to be budgeted for each interim period. In contrast, product cost per unit and variable expenses per unit may be fairly uniform over the entire year. As you would guess, each business develops its own practical solutions to these problems; there's no one general answer that fits all companies.

Accountants understand the need for comparative management control reports (this period versus last or actual versus budget). However, my experience is that most accountants do *not* design internal profit control reports to fit the decision-making thinking used by managers. In my opinion this is a most serious problem.

Profit Control Reports

The typical accounting profit control report closely resembles the external income statement reported to creditors and investors, except in more detail. This won't do. My advice to managers is this: If your internal accounting profit control report looks anything like your external income statement, you'd better start over.

You may have to badger your accountant a little; not all accountants understand that management control and external financial reporting are two very different worlds. But don't allow the accountant to take the easy way out; don't tolerate a more detailed version of your external income statement for internal management control reporting.

Fundamentally, my advice is that the profit profiles developed in previous chapters should be the models for designing internal profit control reports for managers. The external income statement is a very poor model for designing profit control reports for manager. The following quick review of the first ten chapters explains why.

First and foremost, profit margins must be the focus of attention. Recall that profit margin is sales price less product cost and less all variable expenses in making sales. Profit margins absolutely must be reported for each major product or product line in profit control reports to managers. This is very sensitive data, which is not divulged in external income statements. Only total gross profit (after deducting product cost, but before deducting the variable expenses of making sales) is reported in the external income statement. This aggregate number is far removed from the more specific profit margin information needed by managers.

Variable expenses should be divided between those that depend on sales volume versus those that depend on sales revenue. Of course, sales volumes for each major product or product line should be reported. Fixed expenses should be broken down into major components: salaries, advertising, occupancy costs, and so on. Sales capacity should be reported (as well as production capacity for manufacturers). Any change in capacity due to changes in fixed expenses should be reported. What was the incremental cost of the additional capacity, or what was the reduction in capacity relative to the amount of decrease in fixed expenses?

In internal management control reports, changes in operating profit should be analyzed. In particular, the impact of sales volume changes should be separated from changes in sales price, product cost, and variable expenses. If trade-off decisions were made, for example, reducing sales price to increase sales volume, there should be the follow-up analysis in the management control report that tracks how the decision actually worked out. Did sales volume increase as much as expected?

As discussed in Chapter 5, manufacturers have special problems in determining product cost. Internal management control reports should be very clear regarding how idle-production capacity was accounted for in determining product cost. If there were excessive materials or labor costs, these should be separated out; the examples in Chapter 5 illustrate this point.

As Chapter 6 points out, there is a "frustrating fringe" of negative factors that constantly threaten profit margins and bloat fixed expenses. Each of these negative factors should be singled out for special attention in management profit control reports. Inventory shrinkage, for example, should be reported on a separate line, as should sales returns, unusually high bad debts, and so on.

Financial Condition and Cash Flow Control Reports

In contrast to external income statements, the basic structure and content of the balance sheet and cash flow statement in external financial reports are good models for management control reports. The most important management control report is the comparative balance sheet (Please refer to the example in Table 8–1). The manager should keep a close watch on changes in each operating asset and each operating liability; the comparative balance sheet is the best way of doing this.

Sales revenue and expenses drive the operating assets and liabilities of the business. As Chapter 7 explains, changes in every operating asset and liability should be compared with the change in the underlying sales revenue or expense factor that determine the asset or liability. If sales revenue increased 10 percent, did Accounts Receivable go up 10 percent? Why not?

As Chapter 8 explains, changes in the operating assets and liabilities directly affect cash flow from profit. For example, if accounts receivable increase $100,000, cash flow from profit decreases $100,000. Controlling cash flow from profit means controlling changes in the company's operating assets and liabilities. The comparative balance sheet is an indispensable control report for this purpose.

Return on Capital in Control Reports

Internal management control reports should include return on capital measures (See Chapter 9). Return on assets, return on equity, and any changes in the financial leverage factors should be reported. If the business uses the DuPont model for analyzing its return on capital, then this period should be compared against last period, or actual against budget. If the business falls below its ROE goal, there should be a very clear explanation that pinpoints which factors are to blame.

A FINAL WORD

Any experienced manager will tell you that control looks easy in theory, but that it is very difficult in practice. I certainly agree. Good control reports are very important; they supply the feedback information managers need to know in following through on their decisions. But in the final analysis it comes down to good management.

Managers are problem solvers, and many problems do not lend themselves to easy or obvious solutions. Good management starts with good decisions. Control procedures are certainly required. However, the best control in the world can't reverse a bad decision. The main thrust of this book has been to explain techniques of analysis for making good decisions. I hope this book helps you.

INDEX

A

Accounting controls, 177, 178, 179–83
  and AICPA, 180–83
Accounts payable, 139
  and cash flow, 130
  and inventory, 112–13
  prepaid expenses, accrued expenses, 113–14
Accounts receivable, 139
  and cash flow, 127–29, 130
  and sales revenue, 111–12
Accrued expenses, 117, 139
  accounts payable, prepaid expenses, 113–14
Accumulated depreciation, 115, 130–31
Actual output, 63
Adjustments, 92
Administrative/management capacity, 96
AICPA. *See* American Institute of Certified Public Accountants (AICPA)
Allocated amount, 84
Allocation, and fixed expenses, 99–101
Allowances, 92
Alternative minimum tax (ATM), 153
American Institute of Certified Public Accountants (AICPA), 180–83

American Telephone and Telegraph (AT&T), 94
Amounts, calculated and average, 66
Annual percentage rate (APR), 169
Annuity, 169
APR. *See* Annual percentage rate (APR)
Arthur Andersen, 81
Assets, 107, 108, 109
  and capital sources, 139–41
  fixed. *See* Fixed assets
  investment, and future returns, 160–65
  investment profile, 141–48
  net. *See* Net assets
  operating. *See* Operating assets
  See also Return on assets (ROA)
Assets investment profile, 141–48
Associated Press, 73
AT&T. *See* American Telephone and Telegraph (AT&T)
ATM. *See* Alternative minimum tax (ATM)
Auditing Standards Board, 180
Average amount, 66

B

Bad debts, 48
Balance sheet
  comparative, 120–22, 134
  completed, 117–18
  and income statement, 105–19

Balance sheet—*Cont.*
  and profit, 107–18
  and retained earnings, 117–18
Blueprint, decision, 183
Book values, 153, 155
(Boulder) Daily Camera, 73
Break-even chart, 9
Break-even point, 8–11
  computing, 54–55
  and operating loss, 87
Bribes, 95
Budgeting, 179
  and controlling expenses, 186–87
  nature of, 183–84
  profit, 184–86
Burden rate, 73
  overhead, 80–81
Businesses, service, 52–58
Buy, or lease, 165–68

C

Calculated amount, 66
Capacity, 11, 53
  administrative/management, 96
  excess, 96–97
  idle. *See* Idle capacity
  practical sales. *See* Practical sales capacity
  production. *See* Production capacity
  sales. *See* Sales capacity
  and sales volume, 88
Capital
  cost of, and time value of money, 156–74
  and debt and equity, 140
  paid-in, 107
  return on, 139–55, 192
  weighted average cost of, 156, 157–59
Capitalization requirements. *See* Inventory capitalization requirements
Capitalize, 68

Capital lease, 167
Capital sources, and assets, 139–41
Capital sources profile, 141–48
Cash, 139
  and sales revenue and expenses, 111
Cash equivalents, 124, 126
Cash flow, 120–38
  and accounts payable and accounts receivable, 130
  and accounts receivable, 127–29
  control reports, 191–92
  and cost-of-goods-sold expense, 129
  and depreciation expense, 130–32
  and inventory, 129–30
  and operating liabilities, 132–33
  and prepaid expenses, 130
  and profit (operations), 127–33, 133, 135–38
  and sales revenue, 128
  and sales trends, 136–37
  zero, from profit, 133–35
  See also Cash flow statement (CFS)
Cash flow control reports, 191–92
Cash flow statement (CFS), 108, 118, 121, 122–33
  introduction, 122–25
  three parts of, 126–27
  See also Cash flow
Cash price, and credit price, 172–74
Certified Public Accountant (CPA), 179–83
  and AICPA, 180–83
Chandler, Colby, 98
Change
  constant, 16
  fixed expenses, 42–43
  product-cost, 25–26, 37–42
  sales-price, 21–24, 37–42
  sales-volume, 17–21, 37–42
Chrysler Corporation, 8–9, 124
Coca-Cola, 3, 87
Common denominator, 81
  and sales volume, 58–62

Comparative balance sheet, 120–22, 134
Comparative reports, 187–90
Composite number, and product cost, 63
"Consideration of the Internal Control Structure in a Financial Statement Audit," 180
Contribution margin, 8
Control
   accounting. *See* Accounting controls
   management. *See* Management control
   managers, 14, 30
Control reports
   management, guidelines for, 187–92
   profit, 190–91
"Coping with the New Inventory Capitalization Rules," 68
Cost
   of capital, and time value of money, 156–74
   direct labor. *See* Direct labor costs
   indirect. *See* Indirect costs
   manufacturing. *See* Manufacturing costs
   non-direct. *See* Non-direct costs
   period. *See* Period costs
   product. *See* Product cost
   R&D. *See* Research and development (R&D) costs
Cost-of-goods-sold expense, 68, 70, 75, 108
   and cash flow, 129
   inventory and accounts payable, 112–13
Coupons, 92
CPA. *See* Certified Public Accountant (CPA)
Credit cards, 48
Credit price, and cash price, 172–74
Credit sales price, 172
Crutsinger, Martin, 73
Customers, notes receivable from, 168–74

D

Daily Camera, Boulder, 73
Danforth, Douglas, 96
Debt
   bad, 48
   and capital, 140
   and equity, 153–55
Decision blueprint, 183
Decision making, and managers, 3, 14, 30
Denominator, common. *See* Common denominator
Depreciation, accumulated. *See* Accumulated depreciation
Depreciation expense, 85
   and cash flow, 130–32
   and fixed assets, 114–15
Deutsch, Claudia H., 76
Direct labor costs, 67
Discounts, and frustrating fringe, 92
Dollar amount, and sales revenue, 48
DuPont model (pathway), to ROE, 148–52, 192

E

Earnings, retained. *See* Retained earnings
   See also Earnings per share (EPS)
   See also Price/earnings (P/E) ratio
   See also Earnings before interest and tax (EBIT), 145
Earnings before interest and tax (EBIT), 145
Earnings per share (EPS), 154–55
EBIT. *See* Earnings before interest and tax (EBIT)
Effective-interest-rate method, 169
Effects, interaction. *See* Interaction effects
Efficiency, 63
Environmental scan, and managers, 82
EPS. *See* Earnings per share (EPS)

Equations, and balance sheet, 107
Equity
   and capital, 140
   and debt, 153–55
   multiplier, 150
   owners', 107
   See also Return on equity (ROE)
Equity multiplier, 150
EXCEL, 35
Excess capacity, 96–97
Expenses, 107
   accrued. *See* Accrued expenses
   controlling, and budgeting, 186–87
   cost-of-goods-sold. *See* Cost-of-goods-sold expense
   depreciation. *See* Depreciation expense
   fixed. *See* Fixed expenses
   operating. *See* Operating expenses
   prepaid. *See* Prepaid expenses
   and sales revenue, 111
   sales-revenue-dependent. *See* Sales-revenue-dependent expenses
   variable. *See* Variable expenses

F

FASB. *See* Financial Accounting Standards Board (FASB)
Favors, 95
FIFO inventory method, 68
Financial Accounting Standards Board (FASB), 128
Financial condition, and cash flow control reports, 191–92
Financial condition equation, 107
Financial leverage, 144–48
Financing, and cash flow statement (CFS), 126
Finished-Goods-Inventory account, 66
Fixed assets, and depreciation expense, 114–15
Fixed costs, production, 99–100
Fixed expenses, 3–6, 26–27
   and allocation, 99–101
   changes in, 42–43
   non-manufacturing, 100
   and operating loss, 84–86, 89
   and sales mix, 97–101
Ford Motor Company, 111
Form utility, 64
Fortune 500 Industrials, 64
Fringe. *See* Frustrating fringe
Frustrating fringe, 91–97
Full-cost absorption method, 79
Future returns, and asset investment, 160–65

G

GAAP. *See* Generally accepted accounting principles (GAAP)
Generally accepted accounting principles (GAAP), 13
Guiles, Melinda G., 9

H

Historical value, 153

I

Iacocca, Lee, 9, 124
IBM. *See* International Business Machines (IBM)
Idle capacity, 72–76
Income statement, 13–14, 93, 95, 109–11
   and balance sheet, 105–19
Income tax, 152–53
Income tax payable, 117
Indirect cost, 67
Inefficiency, 63
Ingrassia, Paul, 9
Interaction effects, 29

Interest
    simple, 169
    See also Earnings before interest and tax (EBIT), 145
Internal control structure, 180
Internal rate of return, 162
Internal Revenue Service (IRS), and income statement, 13
International Business Machines (IBM), 111
Inventory
    and accounts payable, 112–13
    capitalization requirements, 69
    and cash flow, 129–30
    methods, FIFO and LIFO, 68
Investing, and cash flow statement (CFS), 126
Investment
    asset, and future returns, 160–65
    short-term, liquid, 124, 126
IRS. *See* Internal Revenue Service (IRS)

J

Job-order basis, 64
Journal of Accountancy, 68

K

Kickbacks, 95
Kodak, 98

L

Labor costs, 161, 163
    direct. *See* Direct labor costs
Landman, Robert S., 68
Leader, loss. *See* Loss leader
Lease
    or buy, 165–68
    capital, 167
    operating, 168
Leverage, financial, 144–48

Liabilities, 107, 108, 109, 132–33
    operating. *See* Operating liabilities
LIFO inventory method, 68
Liquidation, 129
List price, 91
Loading, and manager, 90
Loan-payment schedule, 173
    alternative, 168–72
Loser, 82–91
Loss, operating. *See* Operating loss
Loss leader, 99
LOTUS, 35, 42

M

Management control, 14, 30, 177–92
    and accounting controls, 177, 178, 179–83
    control reports, guidelines for, 187–92
    See also Managers
Managers
    and administrative/management capacity, 96
    and cash flow from profit, 135
    and cash flow statement, 118, 124
    and comparative budget sheet, 121–22
    and current product cost, 47
    and decision making, 3, 14, 30
    and environmental scan, 82
    and loading, 90
    and profit patrol, 82
    and profit profile, 14–15, 19
    See also Management control
Manufacturers
    and product cost, 47, 63–81
    versus retailers and wholesalers, 64
Manufacturing cost, 66
    variable, 76–78
Manufacturing-cost profile, 65, 68–72

Margin
  contribution. *See* Contribution margin
  profit. *See* Profit margin
Materials, raw, 67
Melicher, Ron, 150

N

Negative factors, 91–97
  sales-price, 91–94
  sales-volume, 95
  variable-expense, 94–95
Net assets, 116
Net sales price, 93
New York Times, 76, 98, 100
Non-direct costs, 81
Non-manufacturing fixed expenses, 100
Notes receivable, from customers, 168–74

O

Occupancy rates, 96
Operating assets, 139
Operating expenses, prepaid expenses, accounts payable, accrued expenses, 113–14
Operating lease, 168
Operating liabilities, 139
  three, 132–33
Operating loss, 83–91
  computing, 86
Operating profit, 3–6, 11–13
  and classification errors, 68–72
  computing, 7–11
  per unit, 7, 44, 87
Operations
  and cash flow statement (CFS), 126, 127–33
  See also Cash flow
Output
  actual. *See* Actual output
  production. *See* Production output

Overhead, 67
Overhead-burden rates, 80–81
Owners' equity, 107

P

Paid-in capital, 107
Penalty, 92
P/E ratio. *See* Price/earnings (P/E) ratio
Percentage points, of sales capacity, 53–54
Period costs, and product costs, 66–68
Planning, 30
Plant, location and layout, 64
Positioning, of product, 45
Practical sales capacity, 29–30
Prepaid expenses, 139
  accounts payable, accrued expenses, 113–14
  and cash flow, 130
Present value amount, 174
Price
  list. *See* List price
  sales. *See* Sales price
  See also Price/earnings (P/E) ratio
Price/earnings (P/E) ratio, 155
Product, and positioning, 45
Product cost, 46–47
  changes, 25–26, 37–42
  and composite number, 63
  current, 47
  and manufacturers, 63–81
  manufacturing costs and production output, 65–66
  and period costs, 66–68
  and variable-expense negatives, 94–95
Production, excessive, 79–80
Production capacity, 63, 65
  idle, 72–76
Production fixed costs, 99–100
Production output, and manufacturing costs, 65–66

Product line product profile, 97–98, 99, 100
Product profile, product line. *See* Product line product profile
Products, multiple, 80–81
Profile
  assets investment. *See* Assets investment profile
  capital sources. *See* Capital sources profile
  manufacturing-cost. *See* Manufacturing-cost profile
  profit. *See* Profit profile
Profit
  and balance sheet, 107–9
  basics of making, 1–101
  budgeting, 184–86
  cash flow from, 133, 135–38
  and cash flow statement (CFS), 126, 127–33
  control reports, 190–91
  equation, 107
  financial side of, 101–74
  margin, 3–6, 89–91
  operating. *See* Operating profit
  pathway to, 3–15
  patrol, 82–101
  reports, 13
  and sales trends, 136–37
  sensitivity, 16–28
  and zero cash flow, 133–35
  See also Profit profile
Profit profile, 14–15, 18, 19, 21, 22, 23, 24, 25, 26, 27, 30, 32, 35, 36, 38, 40, 41, 43, 141–48
  fine-tuning, 45–62
  and manufacturing-cost profile, 70
  and spreadsheet programs, 35, 42
  See also Profit
Prompt payment discounts, 92

Q

Quantity discounts, 92

R

R&D cost. *See* Research and development (R&D) costs
Rate of return, internal, 162
Raw materials, 67
Rebates, 92
Reports
  cash flow control, 191–92
  comparative, 187–90
  management control, guidelines for, 187–92
  profit control, 190–91
Research and development (R&D) costs, 67
Retailers, versus manufacturers, 64
Retained earnings, 107
  and balance sheet, 117–18
"Retiring Westinghouse Chief Executive Talks of Issues Facing Firms and Managers," 97
Return on assets (ROA), 145, 147, 149, 157–59, 165–68
Return on capital, 139–55, 192
Return on equity (ROE), 143, 144, 146, 147, 148–52, 157–59, 192
Return on sales (ROS), 149, 151
Returns, future, and asset investment, 160–65
Revenue, sales. *See* Sales revenue
ROA. *See* Return on assets (ROA)
Roderick, David M., 76
ROE. *See* Return on equity (ROE)
ROS. *See* Return on sales (ROS)
Rullan, Jose A., 68

S

Sales capacity, 11, 53–54
  practical. *See* Practical sales capacity
Sales discounts, 92
Sales mix
  analysis of, 82–83
  and fixed expenses, 97–101

Sales price
  credit. *See* Credit sales price
  net, 93
  and sales volume, 50–52
Sales-price changes, 21–24, 37–42
Sales-price negatives, 91–94
Sales-price trade–offs, 30–37
Sales, return on (ROS). *See* Return on sales (ROS)
Sales revenue, 107
  and accounts receivable, 111–12
  and cash flow, 128
  and dollar amount, 48
  and expenses, 111
  and sales volume, 46, 53
Sales-revenue-dependent expenses, 47–52
Sales revenue per employee, 96
Sales revenue per square foot, 96
Sales trends, and cash flow from profit, 136–37
Sales volume, 3–6
  and capacity, 88
  common denominator, 58–62
  and sales price, 50–52
  and sales revenue, 46, 53
Sales-volume changes, 17–21, 37–42
Sales-volume negatives, 95
Sales-volume trade-offs, 30–37
Salomon Brothers, Inc., 94
Schedules, loan-payment. *See* Loan-payment schedules
Service businesses, 52–58
Short-term, liquid investments, 124, 126
Simple interest, 169
Special customer discounts, 92
Spreadsheet programs, and profit profile, 35, 42
Statement on Auditing Standards, 180
Statements
  cash flow (CFS). *See* Cash flow statement (CFS)
  income. *See* Income statement

T

Tax
  ATM. *See* Alternative minimum tax (ATM)
  income. *See* Income tax
  See also Earnings before interest and tax (EBIT), 145
Tax Reform Act (TRA), 68, 69, 71, 152
Time-and-price utility, 64
TRA. *See* Tax Reform Act (TRA)
Trade-offs, 29–44, 57–58
  sales-price, 30–37
  sales-volume, 30–37

U

Unearned revenue liability account, 130
Uniform loan payments, 173
Uniform principal reduction, 169, 170, 171
University of Colorado, 150
"U.S. Industry's Unfinished Struggle," 76
USX, 76
Utility
  form, 64
  time-and-price, 64

V

Values, 64
  book, 153, 155
  debt and equity, 153–55
  historical, 153
Variable expenses, 26–27
Variable-expense negatives, 94–95
Variable overhead, 67
Volume, sales. *See* Sales volume

W

Wall Street Journal, 8, 9, 94, 96–97, 155

Weighted average cost of capital,
    156, 157–59
Westinghouse, 96
Wholesalers, versus manufacturers,
    64
Work-In-Process account, 66

Y–Z

"Yellow Light; Chrysler Hits Brakes,
    Starts Saving Money After
    Shopping Spree," 9
Zero cash flow, from profit, 133–35